Christians in a .com World

Focal Point Series

ReViewing the Movies:
A Christian Response to Contemporary Film
by Peter Fraser and Vernon Edwin Neal

Christians in a .com World:
Getting Connected Without Being Consumed
by Gene Edward Veith, Jr. and Christopher L. Stamper

FOCAL POINT SERIES

Gene Edward Veith, Jr., general editor

Christians in a .com World

Getting Connected Without Being Consumed

Gene Edward Veith, Jr.
and
Christopher L. Stamper

CROSSWAY BOOKS • WHEATON, ILLINOIS
A DIVISION OF GOOD NEWS PUBLISHERS

Cover design: David LaPlaca

Cover photo: PhotoDisc™

First printing 2000

Printed in the United States of America

Some of the material in this book has appeared in another form in *World Magazine.*

Library of Congress Cataloging-in-Publication Data
Veith, Gene Edward, 1951-
   Christians in a .com world : getting connected without being
consumed / Gene Edward Veith, Jr. and Christopher L. Stamper
    p. cm. — (Focal point series)
   ISBN 1-58134-218-7 (pbk. : alk. paper)
   1. Internet x Religious aspects —Christianity. 2. Cyberspace—
Religious aspects—Christianity. I. Title: Christians in a dot com world.
II. Stamper, Christopher L., 1972- III. Title.
   BR99.74.V45   2000
   261.5—dc21   00-009617
                                          CIP

15	14	13	12	11	10	09	08	07	06	05	04	03	02	01	00
15	14	13	12	11	10	9	8	7	6	5	4	3	2	1	

Contents

CHAPTER ONE

Introduction: The Latest Frontier

§

Imagine a shopping mall the size of Australia. Or a collection of writings bigger than the Library of Congress, where the books are all scattered on the floor and some appear and disappear without notice. In fact, other people are willing to pay to make sure their books get tossed your way. They fight with one another to get their words in your hands.

Think about a never-never land where anybody can be anyone or anything they want, where present or past conditions matter nothing. Or a political convention where everybody in the planet can give a speech. Or a Turkish bazaar where anything can be bought or sold, both legal and illegal.

Picture a theme park for grown-ups where you can find true love, make a million dollars, or max out your credit cards. Or a hot-air balloon that travels at the speed of light, letting you drop in on any culture or people and study how they live.

All these are metaphors about the Internet, which sprang up seemingly out of nowhere in the 1990s, hooking up millions of people through digital connections and personal computers. This is cyberspace, a placeless realm where one can find the civilization heights of the Renaissance and the Reformation, the moral pit of Sodom and Gomorrah, and every culture's dreams of the future.

Just as Christians latched on to the printing press, so should they grab hold of the Internet for the kingdom of God. The whole universe is His domain, including the world of information translated into data packs, fed through high-speed routers, and sent off on fiber-optic lines. This new technology is a chance to exercise discernment, take some risks, and possibly change the world.

BUY! BUY! SPEND! SPEND! CLICK! CLICK!

Nearly everyone wants a piece of the action. Cyberspace beckons to all races, ethnicities, and belief systems, and each is represented somewhere. Anyone who can read a screen, tap a keyboard, and get an account is welcome. And new tribes of buyers and sellers want to turn those users into customers.

The technology has left people swimming in information. College students wind up with more E-mail than they can read, businesses have instantaneous market information from tracking statistics extracted from customers, and stock traders can risk fortunes by tracking the market minute-by-minute. Those who cook up ways to turn data into dollars (or can make computers deliver it better) can be well rewarded.

The opening of the online frontier is a new gold rush, with unimaginable fortunes being made (and lost) and prospectors scrambling to stake their claims. A rash of dot-com startups lined up to get launched and hit the stock market, with fast-talking CEOs boasting bright Internet ideas, even if the company was without a profit or even a product. These dreams hit a reverse reality check when their stock traded for millions of dollars in hard, real currency.

The oft-hyped e-commerce aspect of the Net is mind-boggling. Everything imaginable from Bibles to canned beets can be found or bought on the Internet. Entrepreneurs adore it, governments hate it, and no one can find everything they're looking for. Many new industries exist that consist simply of online businesses helping online businesses.

Virtual shopping malls have opened in the virtual neighborhoods. The salesman at the door has been replaced by an innocuous-looking blue link to a web site. Online auctioneers take bids on any object imaginable. Just look at Amazon.com, the Seattle-based retailer that went from being a startup bookseller to the embodiment of retailing's future. With no profit but high stock prices, the company leveraged itself farther and farther, expanding from books only into music, video, toys, software, and even tools. It even opened its infrastructure to outsiders via online auctions and what it calls zShops, which allow other retailers to open storefronts on its site.

Superstores are popping up online faster than anyone can build them in the physical world. While they don't require the real estate and upkeep of brick-and-mortar stores, the rivalry is fiercer than in any city. Ironically, the sheer number of players in the market means that margins are plummeting, making profits hard to find. There are seemingly endless competitors offering the same golf clubs, disk drives, and hymnals. In speculative areas, prices can be driven to wholesale cost or lower. Stores gladly lose money today to gain a market share for tomorrow.

All this cutthroat competition means the Net is a buyer's market. The government is still searching for ways to tax the Net, and state and local governments cringe at the idea of lost sales and property taxes. Is all this an opportunity for mindless commercialism and consumerism? Yes, but so is the mail system and every exit on the interstate highways. For people looking for a deal online, the ultimate goal should not be endless spending but improved stewardship. No system for finding the best product at the best price has ever existed before in human history. Such a free economy is working exactly the way Adam Smith thought it would.

E-MAIL, E-COMMERCE, ECONOMY

The digital boom doesn't mean that the Internet is just a destination. For some it can be a career as the Net becomes a bigger and bigger factor in the economy. The stock boom of the 1990s, which might have been impossible without the dot-coms, is just one example. If the Internet was weaned with dreams of freedom, it grows on dreams of free markets. People can surf for goods or for work from anywhere in the world. The result is capitalism unchained.

A simple E-mail account opens the door for knowledge workers to freelance, consult, outsource, contract, and otherwise labor for the highest bidder. Mobility is increased because people can work wherever they are—at home or on vacation. It is mobility while staying where you are. Online auctions turn housewives into steely-eyed traders, bidding on whatever they want and putting the laws of supply and demand directly to work.

In the new economy's offices, company workers thrive in a permanent casual day as utilitarian companies scrap dress and behavior codes in a drive for efficiency not seen since the Industrial Revolution. Those who know how to make computers work are recruited like star athletes and are given stock and higher salaries to jump from company to company. (Who cares if they wear shorts to work? They can write code!)

Keep in mind that the earth-shattering boom came even as the technology was (and is) still growing up. This technology is brand-new, but it's never going away. New applications are dreamed up daily, and the technology keeps getting better, cheaper, and more innovative—opening up even more possibilities and raising more and more questions.

Even if the Net changes the way people work, it doesn't change human nature. It isn't the road to utopia, eternal prosperity, or an easy path to success. The new economy simply expands the options for smart people willing to roll up their sleeves. Work is still work, and a boss is still a boss, even if he doesn't wear a suit and tie anymore. Personal discipline, hard work, and ingenuity are still critical and are still well rewarded in a crazy Net economy.

CALL ME, PAGE ME, E-MAIL ME, TALK TO ME!

Yet the most important communication is not what movers and shakers do with the Net, but what ordinary people say to each other on the Net. E-mail is the lowest common denominator of the online world. To be plugged in means to have an address where one can send and receive messages. Everything else pales in importance. It helps both the loner and the social traveler.

Cheaper than a phone call and easier than a fax machine, E-mail lets people meet and stay in touch who could never connect before. Friendships can survive that would have been blown away by winds of physical circumstance. An accountant in Montana can get help from a computer programmer in India. A kilted Scotsman can find love with a southern belle. And your next chess opponent could as easily come from Russia as from down the block.

Such things would have seemed extravagant, expensive, and downright impossible for most of the twentieth century; yet today they are taken for granted. Nowadays who cares if any of the people in your online Bible study live in the same state?

E-mail is nonintrusive and deceptively simple. It doesn't knock on the door, ring, or interrupt dinner. There's no need to worry about handwriting or special stationery or a trip to the post office. It can have the immediacy of a phone call or the leisure of a vacation postcard. E-mail just sits in the in-box waiting to be read. It can be ignored, devoured immediately, printed out and read the old-fashioned way, or passed around to as many people as you want. E-mail software comes and goes, but the basic format has gone unchanged for years. You input the address of the recipient, add a subject line, type a message, and send. There's hardly a learning curve.

Time, place, and geography have not disappeared, but they have new meanings. While calling someone in the middle of the night might be rude, no one cares about writing or receiving an electronic letter at 2 A.M. They never interrupt anything and can be attended to at one's leisure (and if some social initiative is undesired, a quick tap of the delete key makes it go away).

E-mail has brought the moribund art of letter-writing back to life. It strikes against the dumbing-down trend by requiring some literacy. After all, one must write to do anything. One must also learn to think before typing. Something that might be said by talking on the phone now requires a short essay. Thus many are learning the strengths and weaknesses of their own writing style. E-mail has its own rules for tact, grace, friendliness, and geniality. A few words can cover acts of public boorishness or make a gentleman look like a creep. Something dashed off in the heat of the moment may be totally misinterpreted by someone reading slowly at leisure. But effective writers are learning that the keyboard is mightier than the sword.

Unfortunately, the beauty of E-mail is being endlessly tarnished by the specter of spam, junk E-mail. It piles up in the world's mailboxes, and no hope is in sight. A mid-1999

GartnerGroup survey of 13,000 E-mail users[1] found that 90 percent of users receive spam at least once a week promoting everything from cyber-porn to pyramid schemes to quack health remedies.[2] Almost 50 percent of users get spammed six or more times per week.

Gartner's analysts say that spam increases as one stays with the E-mail account. Unlike paper junk mail, which costs only the sender, spam costs the recipients and service providers in the form of wasted online time, bandwidth, and disk space. Merely entering a chat room or publishing one's address can get a person flooded with crazy ads—and worse, the most degrading pornography. Porn used to be something that you had to actively hunt for on the Web, which made it accessible but easy to avoid. Now, thanks to spam, it hunts for you.

For those who want more direct two-way communication right away, time can stretch in a different direction. That's where E-mail's flashy little brother, the chat client, comes in. People can pop messages back and forth in real time. The trade-off is that while E-mail gives someone a stationery that fits anyone's writing style, chat forces all conversations into bursts of only a few lines.

Chat comes in two flavors, the chat room (where a bunch of people come together like strangers in a cocktail party) and instant messaging (where individuals talk back and forth as if they were on the phone). Either gives people the chance to make friends, do work, or be a complete jerk. With instant messaging, you can see whether or not a contact anywhere in the world is online; and if so, you can pop that person an instant message, complete with a little box for the reply. (Assuming the person on the other side wants to talk.)

America Online streamlined the process with an invention called the "buddy list" and used the leverage to conquer the world of online services. Millions keep little directories of people to greet, converse with, or even harass over the Net. It's simple, cheap, and revolutionary. Whether with private instant messages or in chat rooms open to the public, electronic conversations can go for hours. Everything from business relations to love affairs has been turbocharged this way.

Since electronic messages are almost always both interactive and written down, they can be even more thoughtful and expressive. A strange sense of immediacy hangs over conversations based on pure words, without either facial expressions or vocal timbre. One reason electronic correspondence can be more personal, paradoxically, is because it is more anonymous. Hiding behind a cryptic screen name or a vague electronic identity, a person can express himself with great freedom, free of social conventions, shyness, or embarrassment. (Some avant-garde chat software even lets people play cartoon characters who wander around an on-screen window.) A person is more likely to express unfashionable opinions that might never be heard at the dinner table or the office watercooler. Some culture vultures have waxed loudly about how an individual can drop all real-world characteristics and live as a self-invented being on the Net. This, of course, is not going to be a good thing. If, as has been said, one's true character is how one acts when alone and no one can see, the anonymity of the Internet allows a person's true nature—the sinful nature—to come to the surface and to roam without inhibitions.

For all of the serious friendships developed online, there are also freaks lurking in the chat rooms. Every good conversation on AOL or IRC is matched by a stack of babbling and a dumpster full of real-time sleaze. Finding a good chat is like panning for gold.

Electronic conversation requires a trained ability to quickly weed out garbage and fluff. For all of the serious discussions, personal support, and genuine human relationships made possible through this new technology—even between people who may live on the other side of the world from each other—it is also an occasion for flaming (unrestrained, hateful, and usually obscene invective), virtual sex (erotic, self-stimulating chats), and phony self-presentations on a grand scale (with men pretending to be women, women pretending to be men, and other elaborate scams of identity and deception).

The whole mad scene is expanding beyond the desktop PC. Eventually millions could see their Internet connections, phone lines, and cable TV hookup all combined into one jack in the wall. With a fast enough connection, TV channels and web pages will start to look alike. Entertainment, information, and personal communication are merging now. Though this will create a total media environment, it will not be another collective, homogenizing appeal to the masses, as television has been. It will be more like a private cocoon, for each individual will have access to whatever appeals to his idiosyncratic tastes.

Television used to have only three networks; then cable allowed for fifty (most of which were merely recycling network fare). But the merger of television and the Internet will mean that viewers can watch whatever they want whenever they want it. As broadcasting is replaced by narrowcasting, viewers will be able to choose from a vast menu of options, from classic movies to avant garde experimentation, from Bible studies to New Age seminars, from family fare to the most perverse pornography. The individual will be his own program director, editor, and censor, filtering out whatever he doesn't like, his every whim catered to.

PONDERING THE SITUATION

While all this is often proclaimed as the biggest innovation since Gutenberg's printing press, no one quite understands what it all means. Communication, trade, and information move faster, but moral reality stays the same.

Most of what gets said about the Net is practical—how to get online, E-mail your boss, or start a billion-dollar web site. (Since the medium is so utilitarian, this should be expected.) Occasionally someone pooh-poohs the whole project, calling it complicated, overpromoted, and unprofitable. Sometimes people mock the male-dominated subculture of geeks who work and play at cultivating this new frontier. Journalist Paulina Borsook overreacts to their sometimes anarchist behavior, complaining of "testosterone-poisoned guys with chips on their shoulders and too much time on their hands."[3]

Two groups have presented the most optimistic paradigms about the Internet—the futurists and the Gnostics. The futurists talk of a "New Economy" forever changed because of technology. Meanwhile, the Gnostics proclaim cyberspace as an alternate universe, complete with new politics and new religions. In this libertarian-leftist mix, one can live as an autonomous free citizen with absolute privacy, away from taxation, geography, governments, race, gender, ethnicity, and obscenity laws.

THE FUTURISTS

Futurists take a look at technology, have a great "Oh, Wow!" moment, and then postulate what this means for everyone. Usually the trend is upbeat. The Internet is fulfilling the vision of many who saw the world changing from an industrial society to an information society. TV, satellites, and the telephone all fit a pattern, and the Internet is the next quantum leap.

Alvin Toffler was the popularizer who made this point in a

mass-market way. His 1980 book *The Third Wave* predicted grand shifts in the global economy. Toffler didn't predict the Internet revolution we know, but he explained that inexpensive computers were going to create big changes in the way we live, including access to massive archives, the ability to generate new ideas easily, and even the rise of telecommuting.

Toffler, despite his New Age flavor, helped people focus on the fact that rapid shifts were about to come. The world would be guided by something more than merely the "military-industrial complex" that some people talked about. Toffler stepped into overkill with his talk of a "new civilization," but when people today speak of the digital revolution, they enter into discourse that he helped define.

Today futurists are everywhere. Perhaps today's most pragmatic futurist is a libertarian pundit named George Gilder. Before it was fashionable, he came up with two buzzwords describing the great movements in technology—microcosm and telecosm. *Microcosm* simply refers to the fact that computers get more and more powerful as they get cheaper. *Telecosm* is the exponential rise in value when all these computers come together in a network. In the early 1990s he was saying that these computer networks would be far more important than TV or consumer electronics or the movie industry. When Gilder talks, people don't just listen. They run to their broker, scrambling to buy stocks. When there's a company recommended in his monthly *Gilder Technology Report*, the price often spikes.

Gilder's philosophy of the future centers on a theme—ever increasing bandwidth. Bandwidth refers to the amount of data a computer system can transmit back and forth. When you buy a faster modem, you have more bandwidth and can do more online. When everyone gets more bandwidth, the economy explodes.

So Gilder looks around and finds the companies he thinks will push the bandwidth envelope further. Better Web browsers, faster cellular connections and more efficient corporate networks are the sorts of things that strike his fancy. While he has a reputation for being a stock picker—critics say he encourages speculation and "irrational exuberance"—he's working from a well-grounded methodology.

At one point he criticized conservatives who have a "blanket skepticism" toward technology as if it is just another piece of the modern world to attack. "They're inclined to believe that technology is the machine," Gilder said in a 1992 interview.[4] Thus they unfairly attack what they should embrace.

Numerous others have come along since the Internet boom started, especially as business gurus. On the newsstands, *Wired*, *Fast Company*, *Business 2.0*, and others have all taken up a get-connected-and-get moving attitude. All this is intended to help people figure out what to do with these nifty (and often expensive) tools. Just looking at the ads in the magazine gives one an idea of the energy involved and the pots of gold being chased after.

THE GNOSTICS

While Timothy Leary, the drug guru of the sixties, lay dying of cancer, rumors persisted that he was going to kill himself online. His followers could watch him on a net-camera, and he kept himself turned on and tuned in to this new kind of mind expansion. Leary, knowing that he was dying, conceived the idea of somehow downloading his whole mind onto the Internet. His consciousness would thus be immortal, plugged into the global interconnected consciousness emerging in cyberspace, so that he would attain a virtual eternal life. The whole scheme was a last big publicity stunt before the cemetery and the most obnoxious example of gnosticism hidden behind technological buzzwords.

His cancer-ridden, drug-ravaged body—his "meat machine"—met death the old-fashioned way, and no super-computer has ever been invented big enough to store what is in a human being's mind, let alone his soul. But this sort of con-ceptual possibility is being turned into something people are putting their faith in, so that for many the mystification of the Net is amounting to a new religion. In effect, this expresses New Age metaphysics in terms of tangible, down-to-earth technology.

Some thinkers and artists are proclaiming that we are enter-ing a "post-human" era in which the limits of the body—includ-ing the physical facts of gender, race, appearance, and sexual orientation—will soon be transcended. No one knows who you are online. Your mind alone matters. Your physical body means nothing. The limits of the material universe will be transcended, so that we will exist in a state of true "spirituality" in a universe that we will have created for ourselves.

The reality, of course, is that few people want to live like this. People like having arms and legs and physical identities. What all the verbiage usually describes is dirty talk in chat rooms. This is no substitute for real love and real life.

A fleet of books has tried to explain a religious dimension to the Internet. For example, science writer Margaret Wertheim has written one of the most historical and esoteric, titled *The Pearly Gates of Cyberspace*. She says that the modern idea of the online world revives the supernatural world of Dante's *Divine Comedy* and the medieval cathedrals.

By diminishing the importance of physical space, the rise of the Net makes people rethink their ideas on how the universe works. As the book *TechGnosis* points out, cyberspace has become the religion of taste for an influential few. Writer Erik

Davis thinks that's way cool, telling of a vast pagan feast amid the digital revolution. Skepticism, nihilism, and materialism don't fill that great personal void within, he writes. So our new tools feed on our inner desires and produce "UFOs, Gaian minds, New World Orders and techno-utopias that hover above the horizon of the third millennium."[5] Pseudoscience follows science, and pseudoreligion follows them both.

Such technomystics range from Heaven's Gate leader Marshall Applewhite to Lotus developer Mitch Kapor to Al Gore. Each of them have latched on to the wonder, perplexity, and novelty that comes with new inventions and have steered toward a spiritual goal—salvation from the "noise" of the material world into the "signal" of pure knowledge.

The great gnostic dream rose and fell throughout the 1990s and was reborn on the silver screen in the movie *The Matrix*. It is the tale of Neo, a computer hacker who has stumbled across a dark secret: Normal life is just a computer-generated simulation imposed on us by machines that breed, enslave, and consume us. The character winds up playing Luke Skywalker to Morpheus, an Obi-Wan-like figure, as they fight a bunch of enemy agents who look like the corporate-clad Tommy Lee Jones in *Men in Black*.

Since, according to the movie, the normal world is just a piece of software, nothing "really" exists. In an anarcho-Buddhist fashion, Neo learns he can do everything from spoon bending to zero-gravity kung fu just by using his mind to manipulate the Force, er, the Matrix. The movie piles on the rhetoric about how the usual reality is just a bunch of electrical impulses fed into our brains. A whole pile of science fiction novels by William Gibson, Neal Stephenson, and Bruce Sterling tell similar tales along these lines, constituting the genre known as cyberpunk.

Yet *The Matrix* doesn't entirely invoke a world full of meat machines. The not-so-hidden utopian fantasy of the movie is that once "the system" is overthrown, then people can live free of rules and power games in a real-life, physical world. From a Christian standpoint, such a worldview is completely bogus, but millions are astounded by such mythology. This worldview encourages people to see the Internet as a catalyst into a mountaintop experience. It offers the sense of meaning and the mystical jolt of religion without the drag of morality, discipleship, theology, and the Cross.

GOD, THE REAL WORLD, AND REAL CHRISTIANITY

So where is God in all of this? Cyberspace appears to be a universe wholly created by human beings, enabling them to be oblivious to the real Creator. Yet the world is obviously still His domain. History has moved, but God hasn't.

So what should Christians do? Should they embrace the Amish option and have nothing to do with the new technology because of all the hate and smut and evil? Of course not. For one thing, as society becomes more and more dependent on the Internet, it can hardly be avoided. After all, the Net is a tool, like the phone system and the postal service. Not to mention the fact that Christians are finding the cyberworld extraordinarily useful—in their vocations, on the personal level, and in their ministries.

Christians should use the Net, opting out of the idolatries, tech-worship, and much-ballyhooed paradigm shifts that pale before the biblical worldview. In fact, the Net can be used to promote a Christian view of the real world.

Meanwhile, Christians must protect their families, their children, and themselves from the pedophiles, predators, con artists, and pornographers who have established a major presence in cyberspace. With such a burden, one may wind up wondering if the Amish have the right idea after all. But it need not be that way.

One of the purposes of this book is to demystify the Internet in a jargon-free way that speaks to nontechnical people. When the children of Israel were wandering in the desert, they fell into serious sin, which was punished by a plague of poisonous snakes. At God's direction, Moses used his Bronze Age technology to construct a bronze serpent on a pole. God provided that if anyone bitten by a snake would look at the bronze serpent, he would be healed—a startling typological proclamation of Christ, who bore in His body lifted up on the cross all human sin, the punishment it deserves, and the curse of the Satanic Serpent himself. "And as Moses lifted up the serpent in the wilderness, even so must the Son of Man be lifted up, that whoever believes in Him should not perish but have eternal life" (John 3:14-15, NKJV).

But in time, as the Israelites settled into apostasy, even this evangelistic work of art was turned into an idol, interpreted according to the line of their snake-worshiping neighbors. When Hezekiah became king, however, he worked to stamp out idol worship and bring the nation back to the true God. This included dealing with the relic from Moses' day, which did not, we may regret, include putting it in a museum. Modern translations obscure the significance of exactly what he did, but the reading from the *Authorized King James Version* has good support in the original Hebrew: "He removed the high places, and brake the images, and cut down the groves, and brake in pieces the brazen serpent that Moses had made: for unto those days the children of Israel did burn incense to it: and he called it Nehushtan" (2 Kings 18:4). "Nehushtan" means "a bronze thing." Hezekiah destroyed it, but to fully stamp out idolatry, he also needed to demystify it. "This is a piece of bronze," he was saying. "Yes, it is a wonderful relic of our history, and, yes, it is a wonderful work of art with an evangelistic message. But it isn't magic, it isn't something to worship, and we dare not let it lead us astray. It is just a piece of metal."

The prophets were always doing this, trying to bring the people back from idolatry. "This image isn't a god; it's a piece of wood. You build your fires out of this kind of thing. There isn't anything in this object that will save you, nor is there anything in it to be afraid of." (See, for example, Isaiah 44:12-20.)

There are human limits to all technology. In the old *Wonderful World of Disney* TV show in the early 1960s, Tomorrowland would project what the next century, specifically the year 2000, might bring. All of our nutritional needs would be met by pills and freeze-dried nutritional packets, we were told. But it will never happen. Human beings will always like to eat real food. The Tomorrowland landscape was one of concrete and plastic, with round houses on stilts in the air, with nature nowhere to be found in this triumph of scientific ingenuity. But as a matter of fact, now that we have passed the year 2000 we are restoring Victorian buildings, living in new houses that look like old houses, and insisting that our cities provide lots of green places. Human beings, for all of their modernist pretensions, have a need for beauty, history, and nature.

By the same token, human beings have a need for objective reality. They will never escape their human condition, no matter how much they play at it. They will never fully withdraw into a virtual reality they have made, even if they would like to. The real uses of the Internet are those that have ramifications in real life, whether they lead to making money or to making marriages. And the real world is the domain of God.

One of the disappointments being registered about the new technology is that it has not really had much of an impact on education. For all the hype and all the mega-investment in equipment made by school boards, the computer labs are not really doing much beyond word processing, E-mail, and allowing the students to play lots of games. Reading and writing scores are way down, and science education, for all of our infatuation with technology, is in even worse shape. Unless the curriculum works, computers are a waste of money.

Certainly the educational potential of the Internet has hardly been tapped, but all of these information systems, so far, have not made young people more knowledgeable. As one educator said, giving a child a piano will not make him a musician. And giving a child a pencil—or a word processor—will not make him a writer. The old educational tasks and the human condition with all of its limitations, sufferings, and yearnings remain the same.

The point is, technology is a tool. The tool's value depends on what one does with it. From a Christian perspective, the Internet opens up vast potential for evangelism. It is possible to communicate with people around the world without regard for borders or anti-Christian laws. It is a way for Christian thought to enter the marketplace of ideas without being restricted by intellectual gatekeepers that have for the last century excluded the biblical point of view. Or it is possible to use the Internet as a black hole of withdrawal, self-deception, and vice.

Of course, the Internet is not a tool like a hammer or a skill saw. It is a tool that we can use, but it is also a tool that can use us. Dealing as it does with information, language, and thought itself, the Net can shape our thinking and our experiences in complex ways, sometimes without our realizing it. But essentially, like all tools, it becomes an extension of us. In fact, the Net extends what we really are.

In the ultimate entertainment center—which is coming, as has been said, with the integration of television, computers, and the Internet—when every taste can be indulged, the vulgar will be vulgar still. In fact, vulgarity will be unbounded, reaching depths of vulgarity not yet seen (and you thought it couldn't get worse). But good tastes can be indulged as well, tapping into great works of meaning, morality, and insight currently unavailable on the mass wasteland of television.

The challenge for the Christian will be, first, to sometimes leave this entertainment immersion in order to visit one's sick neighbor down the street. It will also be the Christian's challenge to resist the temptations to which one's sinful nature is heir. Christians have often thought of sin as if it is something they can stay away from. Evils are external, a contaminant to stay clear of. On one level, this is a valid way to look at evil, avoiding the occasion and the temptation for sin, and it is important to protect one's children and even one's culture from the presence of corruption. But ultimately, as Jesus Himself warns, it is not what comes from outside that makes a man unclean, but what comes out of a man's heart. "For out of the heart come evil thoughts, murder, adultery, sexual immorality, theft, false testimony, slander" (Matthew 15:19). That catalog, as a matter of fact, sounds like a pretty comprehensive list of the uncleanness found on the Internet.

So it will be important for Christians in this digital age to internalize virtue—that is, to grow in sanctification through the life-changing faith in Christ. Discipleship is a survival skill. The Church, God's Word, the sacraments, doctrine, worship—in the real world—will be foundational, as they have always been, but especially in a climate in which everything solid, material, and objective seems to evaporate away.

In a medium in which we are deluged with unfiltered information, so that truth is all mixed up with urban legends, gossip, hoaxes, lunacy, and lies, the danger becomes information overload, disorientation from an indiscriminate sensory and intellectual assault. For the information to be meaningful, we need to process the deluge through a filter, so we can sort out what is valuable from what is worthless. Some people are trying to design software to serve as the gatekeeper we really need after all. But ultimately Christians grounded in God's Word can become their own filters. Having a biblical worldview will give them criteria, standards, and discernment, so they can function in this new sea of information without being washed away.

The Spreading of the Net

The History of
Where We Are

CHAPTER TWO

What Hath God Wrought:
The History of the Computer

෧

A critical fact in the world of 1801," observes Stephen
Ambrose in his account of the Lewis and Clark expedition,
"was that nothing moved faster than the speed of a horse. No
human being, no manufactured item, no bushel of wheat . . . no
letter, no information, no idea, order, or instruction of any kind
moved faster. Nothing ever had moved any faster."[1] America
then was a great society, but it was "a society whose technology
was barely advanced over that of the Greeks. The Americans of
1801 had more gadgets, better weapons, a superior knowledge
of geography, and other advantages over the ancients, but they
could not move goods or themselves or information by land or
water any faster than had the Greeks and Romans."[2]

It took Meriwether Lewis three days to go from Boston to
New York, ten days to go from Jefferson's Virginia home,
Monticello, to Philadelphia. His exploration of the Louisiana
Purchase, which took him to the Pacific Northwest, took three
years. And information traveled just as slowly. In the War of

1812, men fought and died in the Battle of New Orleans without realizing that a peace treaty had already been signed. Letters, military orders, business requests, and news sometimes took months to arrive. The early newspapers consisted mostly of essays, opinions, local information, and, at best, long-after-the-fact hearsay about far-off events. It took months for Americans to learn who had been elected President.

But by the time of the Civil War, the railroad and the steamship had been invented and installed, dramatically shrinking space and time. Information could now be transmitted instantaneously by means of the telegraph.

Samuel Morse was a devout Christian. He was also an artist. One of the first in the New World to make a living from being a painter, Morse is considered one of the best American portrait artists. With his artistic creativity, coupled with his fascination with the newly discovered principles of electricity, he conceived of the idea of using electricity, wires, and the principles of magnetism to transmit coded messages. On May 24, 1844, on thirty-seven miles of line he had strung between Baltimore and Washington, he was ready to give it a try. The first message he tapped out was a Bible verse: "What hath God wrought!" (Numbers 23:23). What Samuel Morse had wrought with, as he believed, God's help was the Information Age. Almost overnight the whole world became wired.

Though the telegraph—with its Morse code, specialized operators, and the need to go to a particular office to send and receive messages—seems clumsy by today's standards, it was revolutionary. Messages that once took months to deliver now took seconds. Civil War generals could convey orders, orchestrate complex troop movements, and transmit up-to-the-minute intelligence instantaneously with the help of the telegraph. Word of casualties got to the families at once with a dreaded telegram.

But also businesses could take orders and communicate to distant factories. Police and fire departments could now coordinate their efforts. Stock tickers opened up Wall Street to the rest of the country. Local papers became international newspapers as stories from around the world came over the wire. The Associated Press was founded only four years after Samuel Morse sent his first message, and now a small-town newspaper in Missouri could report daily events from Washington, London, or Paris.

It all happened very fast. Similarly, in our own century computers have risen to the fore in only fifty years. The Internet was first switched on, in its embryonic form, in 1969, though ordinary people did not go online until two or three decades later, a process that, once it got started, seemingly happened overnight.

But changes that seem to happen overnight actually turn out to have a long history. Technological revolutions are prepared for and are the sum of many small discoveries and human factors that suddenly come together into something remarkable. One strain of the Internet's lineage is the telegraph. Another is the computer. Telephone and television play their part, as do philosophers playing with symbolic logic, military generals, government bureaucrats, and crazed college students. And as far as we have come, the changes, from similarly diverse sources, keep coming.

THE COMPUTER

Hardly anyone in A.D. 1000 could have imagined that people by the end of the millennium would buy plug-in electronic brains. How could anyone even explain the concept? And yet, way back in Y1K they had the beginnings of what would come. They had a computing machine called the abacus. By clicking beads around, people could do math problems and manage a few business transactions. It was simple, could be easily replicated and easily learned, and lasted centuries.

To this day, if you go into a shop in Asia or the former Soviet Union, the storekeeper might add up your tab by counting ten and hundred beads on an abacus. It works just as well as a cash register or a calculator, and it works from a similar principle. Plus it has many features people still desire from a computer: It uses little energy, works fast, and is easily portable.

After a fit of brainstorms and ideas over the ages, Blaise Pascal gave the world an early taste of processing power. Pascal was a seventeenth-century genius who pioneered probability theory, did the original math for conic sections, and developed the whole field of hydrostatics and the study of atmospheric pressure—including the invention of the vacuum pump and the syringe. He was also a devout, profoundly thinking Christian. He became associated with the Jansenists, a group of French Catholics who believed that salvation was by grace alone and other "Reformation" ideas that would soon cause Jansenism to be outlawed by the Roman Catholic Church. A true "Renaissance man" in the wide scope of his interests and abilities that extended throughout the liberal arts (as was Samuel Morse), Pascal was not only a scientist, a mathematician, and an engineer, he was also a creative writer and a theologian. Pascal was a brilliant satirist, lampooning the Jesuits for their moral rationalizations and their attacks on his faith; and his *Pensees*, or "Thoughts," are one of the most profound apologetic works of Christian literature ever written.

When Pascal was nineteen, he wanted to help his father, a city administrator, figure taxes. So he dreamed up and constructed a machine that could do the math. It consisted of gears and cranks and was totally hand-operated, but it was the first digital calculator, the prototype of the computer.

The device, built in the 1640s, was called the Pascaline. It could add numbers up to eight digits and do subtraction. It looked like a brass rectangular box with a series of dials running across it. The Pascaline was big news but hard to use. One problem was that the French currency was not based on 10, making calculating difficult. Only about fifty Pascalines were made before lack of demand brought the project to a halt. Still, a few models actually were sold as late as the early 1850s.

Over the years others tried to tinker with the Pascaline, but a new wave of innovation came in the 1800s. Incandescent light bulbs, telegraph lines, and typewriters were all in the works, all of which would become key pieces to the puzzle.

Early in the nineteenth century, Joseph-Marie Jacquard invented the punch card to control silk looms. By punching the card with holes, one could send instructions to a machine—the same way the roller that controls a player piano works. With punch cards, data could be stored and brought back later. Someone could write a set of instructions to perform the same operations on different sets of cards. Punch cards were an important innovation in the Industrial Revolution, though in our terms they were slow, tedious, and a real pain if spilled on the floor. But they would make computer programming possible.

The first to have grand plans for the punch card was English math professor Charles Babbage. He started building a steam-powered, locomotive-sized invention called the difference engine in 1822. It was intended to generate mathematical tables without using teams of number-crunchers with pen and paper. After ten years he gave up on the difference engine and designed something similar, the analytical engine, the first stab at a programmable computer. Unfortunately, construction was stopped by Babbage's death in 1830.

TOWARD TODAY

The next milestone created IBM, the big blue name that would dominate the industry for decades. In the late nineteenth century, the government offered a competition for the best ideas that would help tabulate the mountainous data accumulated in the growing nation's census. MIT lecturer Herman Hollerith, who devised a way to use punch cards to store census data and to manipulate them mechanically, won the competition for a new tabulating scheme. His machines cut a decade's worth of head counting down to a year of work. By sorting the cards, statisticians could compile population data easily for the first time.

Hollerith saved the government five million dollars, and soon he had a hit on his hands, with orders for his punch card machine coming in from as far away as Canada, Norway, and Russia. His Tabulating Machine Company was founded in 1890 and would become International Business Machines in 1924. Decades later IBM was still using punch cards to control giant mainframes, and for years its eighty-column format was an icon of technological power in the days before floppies and CD-ROMs.

That first five million dollars saved by Hollerith's innovation was the birth of a new idea—that information could be used to save and make money. In Hollerith's time his tabulating machine was just one cog in the Industrial Revolution. It would take a long time for the industrial world to grasp that lesson because the technology was so big and expensive. As processing slowly developed, a world of other technological changes hit; cars, planes, and household appliances rocked the world, leaving people wondering what would come next.

An important bit of speculation came in 1924 when Czech author Karel Capek produced the play *R.U.R*, which popularized the idea of robots. These were machines programmed to do boring tasks. Naturally, in the story they all went nuts and destroyed humanity. This launched the ever-present debate about people being enslaved by technology and computers replacing people—and this was before technology and computers were even capable of it.

With World War II, the various strains began coming together. Another IBM genius, Howard Aiken, invented the electronic calculator in 1944. Considered the first digital computer, it weighed five tons and made a terrible racket. The first real commercial computer, UNIVAC, arrived in 1951. For the next few decades computers were huge, expensive monstrosities that were only thought valuable to science, industry, and academia.

Computers were still mostly punch-card dependent, usable only by experts who had to master arcane programming languages and who could make sense of the raw math these room-sized machines churned out. But the technology was developing to make them smaller, faster, more powerful, and more usable. The transistor, a set of tiny electronic switches, had been invented in 1947; in 1958 the first transistorized computer was designed by Seymour Cray (who would, much later, become famous for his "Super Computers"). This paved the way for the replacement of bulky vacuum tubes with miniature electronics that could store and manipulate data by means of electronic circuits, instead of using punch cards. Only a year later, in 1959, the computer chip was patented, which meant that integrated circuits could be printed on tiny pieces of silicon, then packed into circuit boards, resulting in a huge jump in memory and capability—not to mention lower prices.

But it was not until 1971 that this capability was fully realized, when Intel created the microprocessor. This was a chip that could itself be programmed, performing math and logic functions that could then be stored on other chips. That 4004 chip is a direct ancestor of today's Pentium chip and was originally developed for business calculators. It was small, fast, and cheap. Computers could now be affordable, brought out of the realm of the elite onto the desktop of the masses.

BILL'S BONANZA

The first home computer was made by Altair in 1975, the same year, significantly, that Bill Gates founded Microsoft Corporation, whose operating software could make it all happen. Then more models of home computers came out from Commodore, Radio Shack, Sinclair, Atari, and others. Stephen Wozniak and Steven Jobs introduced the even more user-friendly Apple in 1977. Hard to use and weak by today's standards, all of these computers gave the world a feel for what was possible.

Once the first major spreadsheet program, VisiCalc, came in 1979, more businesses wanted computers. When businesses realized what this technology could do for them, the bright future of microcomputers was guaranteed. Businesspeople could see how by adjusting rows, columns, and formulas of data, they could keep better records and cook up all sorts of statistics faster than they'd ever dreamed. Once a competitor turned to computers, everyone else in that industry had to have it. Within decades the entire business world tossed out its trusty typewriters and adding machines and bought desktop computers and bit-crunching networks. Massive information technology departments sprang up, full of techie types working away to keep everything going.

The real hardball began when IBM, the granddaddy of them all, was lured into the market in 1981 with its first personal computer. Big Blue never understood the PC revolution until too late. It created the standard used by over 90 percent of desktop computers today, only to lose control of the market. IBM wanted its original Personal Computer to ship in a year; so it built a Frankenstein contraption of parts from various manufacturers, notably Intel's processor. Enter Bill Gates and Microsoft, which scored a contract to write an operating system called the Microsoft Disk Operating System—MS-DOS—for the personal computer. IBM didn't take exclusive rights to the product, leaving Microsoft to sell DOS to other vendors. This would make Gates the richest man in the world.

IBM's PC was a big hit, and other manufacturers took notice. Clone makers popped up, imitating IBM's designs, tossing together similar parts running Intel's chips, and making use of Microsoft's operating system. Originally these were low-budget affairs that didn't always work, but over the years upstarts like Compaq, Dell, and Gateway have beaten IBM at its own game.

In the meantime, applications multiplied. Not just numbers but words could be processed and stored electronically. Color monitors made the computer environment an increasingly visual one, especially when in 1985 Microsoft borrowed an experimental icons and graphic organization from Xerox and Apple and turned it into the Windows operating system.

Another revolution came with Pong, which Atari introduced in arcades in 1972. The upstart company almost single-handedly turned video games into an industry and helped put computers in the living room. Many people who build today's web sites were playing Pong or Centipede or Missile Command years ago. By the 1990s computers were regularly serving up 3-D animation, making possible not only games that aspired to "virtual reality" but sophisticated industrial and scientific modeling.

Innovation was fueled both by demand and the constant availability of faster processors. Every few months newer, faster microchips hit the market, upping the ante on PC power and making the computer that was once state of the art that much closer to obsolescence. Intel and competitor Advanced Micro Devices constantly release ever faster models that leave their predecessors in the dust. And since the software is written to take advantage of the latest hardware, the result is a sort of unplanned obsolescence. That's why a computer you buy today will soon be functionally obsolete, requiring the purchase of a new machine that runs the current software.[3] Since a $3000 super-system is on its way to being an expensive small boat anchor, equipment turns over every few years. This may not seem fair, but it accelerates the dynamism of the industry.

According to what has been formulated as Moore's Law, computer speeds double and prices are cut in half every eighteen months. That means chip and software development never stops, with endless new versions always around the corner. The constant flow of technology makes people hungrier for more and better all the time. So the upgrades keep flowing.

POWERING ON TO THE FUTURE

What became of IBM? Big Blue fell behind in sales for years and yanked the Aptiva, the direct descendant of their original PC, out of stores in 1999. The computers stayed available only through ibm.com. Other manufacturers outmaneuvered IBM on similar machines. By the early 1990s, IBM could no longer dictate the machines' future. Clones became so hot that they weren't clones anymore. At first they were "IBM compatible," and then people stopped thinking in terms of Big Blue. Now the systems are just "PCs," made by former cost-cutter outfits like Dell, Compaq, and Gateway. Yet IBM's tactical blunder left a nearly universal standard on the desktop—the operating system sold by Bill Gates.

What matters with a PC is continuity and compatibility more than brand name. Can my computer read the same files as my secretary's? Can my kids play the same games as their friends? This meant there was a need for a standard operating system so that different computers could all run the same programs. Microsoft's operating systems, DOS and Windows, became the common denominator. These weren't the greatest products ever created, but they were good enough for most people. Since practically every major software package is released for PCs running Windows, people tend to buy the same type of configuration time and again. So Bill Gates with Microsoft became the colossus of the computer industry.

As for IBM, the price of PCs crashed in 1997, leaving scads of good PCs selling for under $1,000. IBM simply wasn't nimble enough to maneuver and so lost a lot of money. IBM's Personal Systems Group lost nearly $1 billion in 1998 alone. So to cut out a lot of middlemen, the Aptiva business went online.[4] Hundreds of employees were laid off. Sometimes just being high-tech isn't enough.

Once the PC became a consumer item, people started considering variations. What once filled a room shrank to fit on a desk and then shrank to fit on a lap or in the palm of a hand. Some promoted wearable PCs for those who want to escape from sitting behind a desk but find a laptop too bulky. For industrial uses, these started as full-size PCs that were heavy and bulky and fit around the body like a bulky version of Batman's utility belt. They evolved into devices weighing less than a pound. As such products become more mainstream, we could see more people wanting a hard drive wired to their heads. People could check their E-mail or zap aliens while jogging or sitting on a bus. For techno-isolation, wearables have the old-fashioned Walkman radio beat hands down.

Toy-making giant Mattel inked a deal in 1999 to sell Barbie and Hot Wheels computers. Instead of the usual beige box, kids get brightly colored looks of the company's cash cow product lines. So instead of putting a computer into a toy, why not make a computer into a toy? The Barbie PC, like the 1990s cult favorite iMac, is an example of boutique marketing: Take an ordinary product, add something cool, and give it a new ad campaign. Instead of Ford Mustangs and Cadillac Eldorados, falling prices are causing computer shoppers to turn to the computer equivalent of Geo Metros and VW Beetles. Now people are often buying second and third machines so Mom, Dad, and Junior can check their E-mail at the same time.

In the meantime, as the PC industry was growing, envious eyes started glancing at Microsoft. Some hated the way it controlled so much of the software industry. Others just hated the fact that Microsoft crashes all the time. Many started asking questions: Does Microsoft succeed by serving customers (as it claims)? Or is it an 800-pound-gorilla waging a take-no-prisoners fight to dominate the competition?

As a result, Bill Gates and company were forced to fight a massive antitrust lawsuit from the Justice Department and twenty states. Attorney General Janet Reno claimed Microsoft's "choke hold" on competitors denied consumers important choices about how they buy and use computers. This was the most publicized antitrust case since the AT&T suit that brought down the Bell System.

The Justice Department charged that the world's biggest software company had played an assortment of dirty tricks on the way to the top. Microsoft fought back, arguing it was defending its right to innovate. For the government, the final straw was merging Microsoft's Internet Explorer (IE) browser into the Windows 98 operating system. The government called that an illegal "tying" of separate products, while Microsoft contended its browser is "integrated," a seamless part of its operating system that allows it to work more perfectly with the Internet (the story of whose origin will be the subject of a later chapter).

Since Windows controls desktop PCs, virtually everyone winds up looking at the Web through a window built by Microsoft, which supposedly wins the right to dictate standards and positioning on the Net. Since about 90 percent of all computers in 1999 ran Windows, the argument goes, any other software for navigating the World Wide Web (especially Netscape) could become obsolete fast. Gates says that his company wants to make good products for people, not try to chill competition or take over the Internet. As technology grows, Windows grows. Internet features in operating systems are as logical a step as installing code that reads CD-ROMs. "The government should not stand in the way of logical and useful technological progress," Gates said in written testimony in 1998 before the Senate Judiciary Committee.

Late in 1999, old-fashioned regulations bit Microsoft. U.S. District Judge Thomas Penfield Jackson sided with Janet Reno's argument that Bill Gates's empire stifled innovation and hurt consumers by limiting choices and inflating prices, especially by bundling Internet Explorer into Windows. Like the Standard Oil trust of years ago, the boys in Redmond, Washington, had to pay.

This means America's richest man was forced into war for his Windows—even though he golfed with Bill Clinton, invited Al Gore to a party at his mansion, and gives money to causes like international population control.

True, Microsoft took over the software industry. But if their products didn't meet the needs of desktop customers, people would be running something else today. The computer industry changes so radically that these actions are a huge waste of time. The government's responsibility is to uphold the rule of law, not to reengineer the future of technology. Microsoft is huge, but it doesn't own the world. Except for grabbing browser dominance, Microsoft lagged behind as an Internet power through the 1990s. Competitors were already looking to a post-Windows world, such as the paradigm of "pervasive computing," which puts Internet access wherever one needs it with or without a desktop PC.

LINUS'S FOLLY

In the meantime, as Microsoft braced for being picked apart by a federal court, a feisty competitor in a red hat danced, full of dreams about smashing Windows. An operating system called Linux attracted devoted backers, claiming it can run PCs with more flexibility and fewer crashes. Super-powerful and completely free, anybody in the world can download a copy off the Internet and install it or even change it. This operating system was developed in the early 1990s by a Finnish student named Linus Torvalds and spread like wildfire through techie circles. Linux resembles an old standby named UNIX (hence the name), and computer geeks by the millions have built the operating system into a grassroots movement.

Since Linux's source code was freely available too, programmers could customize their computers like a car nut soups up a '66 Mustang. Thus an army of volunteer programmers who share their tricks with one another is constantly improving it. Others sell boxed copies complete with technical support.

Linux itself has a following that resembles a political movement. Its supporters are split into factions debating whether to sell out Linux to big corporations who want to market it and keep the profits. What once was the domain of techies and hippy-dippy techno-dreamers is turning into something powerful. International Data Corporation said that Linux made up about 17 percent of the software shipped for business PCs in 1998. Yet while Linux has kept getting better, it is still an operating system by the geeks, for the geeks, and of the geeks. The software is notoriously hard to install and operate. A kid could bypass college and launch his career in computers by simply learning how to work Linux.

But the very concept of a stand-alone operating system loaded into an individual computer may itself soon become obsolete. Before the Web came, as we noted, Windows and its predecessor, DOS (disk operating system), were a de facto standard that allowed people to move information from machine to machine. But Internet standards work regardless of the operating system. So who needs Windows to check his E-mail? The computer may well develop into an empty appliance, like the television set, that simply taps into the various programs, functions, and applications broadcast over the Internet.

WHAT IS COMING?

The digital conquest of society has just begun. As a medium, it is just getting close to where television was in its *I Love Lucy* stage. So where is it going?

Computers and modems are getting faster. Fiber optics and broadband transmission technologies are conveying more and more data. The merger of the Internet with television—and with Hollywood and the recording industry and the publishing business—is already happening.

Some developers dream of online invisibility. They want the Internet not to dominate our lives, as it sometimes seems to today, but to fade into the background. The Internet will direct information to the user instead of making the user the servant of his computer.

Eventually some developers would like to get more of the Net off the desktop computer altogether. Cell phones, car computers, and hand-sized personal assistants will be able to access documents. Intelligent devices like game machines, stock tickers, electronic checkbooks, and digital shopping carts would perform one task without requiring computer literacy. This sort of invisibility means total access to information and computer services at all times, but without it being such a big deal.

In time, being on the Net won't be so unusual. The point of pervasive computing is that hardware and software must reduce the number of steps required to obtain some information. Today, for instance, many web sites offer driving directions. You can type in any two addresses in the United States, then print a map and explicit directions ("turn right on Main Street"). But for the lost driver motoring around some unfamiliar suburb, running home to get online isn't an option. So in-dash navigational systems using a wireless web connection are beginning to take up the slack.

Pervasive computing's most obvious entrance point is the cell phone. Future models will be more like portable desks, and the Internet will be inescapable. Everything from cookbooks to calendars to cattle futures will be available by reaching in your pocket.

Former Apple vice president Donald Norman took pen in hand to describe how he wants desktop computers to go away. In *The Invisible Computer* he argued that they are too intrusive, too big, too noisy, and too time-consuming. Our machines should meet our demands, not vice versa. "People are analog, not digital; biological, not mechanical," he exclaims. "It is time for a human-centered technology, a humane technology." Norman's alternative is to replace PCs with "information appliances" that are as nonintrusive as a wristwatch or air conditioning.

Such products include today's digital cameras, personal organizers, and digital phones. They're fun, they do what we want, and they don't take over. For Norman, now an executive with Hewlett-Packard, they are the future. Instead of big-box, single-function devices, they will be carried in briefcases, hidden in our eyeglasses, and even embedded in our furniture. And a lot of them won't be powered by Microsoft and Intel. A new generation of high-tech business success is just starting. "Properly built, properly deployed technology makes people smarter than we would otherwise be," Norman explains. "The problem lies in the word 'properly.'"

He says that right now too much of the computer market is run by "aging teenagers" building the muscle cars of the desktop. They make machines for early adopters, people enthralled with technology or with heavy-duty technological needs. And the PC that results is too much like a Swiss Army Knife. "Of all the umpteen things it does," says Norman, "none of them are done particularly well."5 That must change, he says, or the information revolution will plod along for decades.

The PC probably isn't as bad as Norman describes. After all, there's something to be said for that one-size-fits-all machine that can run an endless variety of software. Still, Norman understands one bit of wisdom very well: Most people don't buy computers just to play with a digital toy. They buy them to do something, like writing E-mail or doing homework or playing chess. Technology is a means, not an end.

ISN'T IT LOVELY?

Another speculator, David Gelernter (a Yale computer scientist who was nearly blown to bits by the anti-technology Unabomber in 1993), says that a machine of beauty is a joy forever. Just as people seek elegance in art, architecture, and music, so they seek *Machine Beauty* (the name of his book) in hardware and software. "A single programmer alone at his keyboard can improvise software machines of fantastic or even incomprehensible complexity," he writes. "Imagine what kind of palaces people would live in if all you needed to do were to draw a blueprint, hand it to a machine, and see the structure realized automatically at the cost of a few drips of electricity."[6]

Gelernter harkens back to the day of Bauhaus, a German design school that searched for the ultimate combination of form and function. A well-designed device, be it a chair, a car, or a computer (or even the Hoover Dam), is as beautiful as a painting—even if the creators don't think of their work in those terms. An example of this elegance is the graphical interfaces that run today's PCs and Macs. Xerox first developed this device in the early 1970s and eventually brought click-and-drag computing to middle America. Instead of typing in a variety of obscure commands, we can drive our machines by clicking pictures with a mouse.

On the other hand, Gelernter hates physical computer design. He says today's hardware wastes space and gives the user a mouse without a pad. "We ought to start teaching [artists like] Velazquez, Degas, and Matisse to young technologists right now on an emergency basis," he writes.[7]

Gelernter's ideas are a healthy corrective to the all-too-prevalent notion that computers have to be sterile and utilitarian. Instead of stripping us of our humanity, new technology opens doors of creativity. The technological revolution means more than information. As Mr. Gelernter says, "Great technology is beautiful technology."[8]

As machines become more powerful, they become smaller and open up new applications beyond mere word processing, spreadsheets, and video games. Some say the future of computers will be like the present-day world of electricity—invisible. When you need something, you flip a switch without thinking of the power lines and transformers. It feels like there's nothing but net.

Whatever happens next, it is evident that future technology will be as different from today's as today's is from the first lab experiment. But what we do with it is our problem.

WHAT HATH GOD WROUGHT!

It is surely significant that the words that inaugurated the wiring of the world—linking people by linking machines, enabling language to obliterate space and distance—were from the Word of God. Samuel Morse, who has been described as America's Leonardo—a master of both art and science, and who was in addition a pious Calvinist—used as his text to transmit over his newly invented telegraph a passage from the book of Numbers.

That was a curious choice. The Gentile prophet Balaam had been pressured by the Moabites to pronounce a curse on the newly freed and migrating children of Israel. But instead, being attuned to the true God, he kept blessing them. In the course of things, the word of the Lord came to the bottom line: "Surely there is no enchantment against Jacob, neither is there any divination against Israel: according to this time it shall be said of Jacob and of Israel, What hath God wrought!" (Numbers 23:23, KJV).

In the *King James Version*, the last sentence is not a question—as it was sometimes rendered in the early reports of the message—but an exclamation, rendered in the NIV as "See what God has done!" The point seems to be that curses and occult powers will not work against God's people. Those people's strength and security and salvation come not from themselves, in which case they would be highly vulnerable, but from what

God has done. This is a statement of the Gospel. Christianity is not a matter of what we do, but of "what God hath wrought"—namely, His Incarnation in Christ, Christ's death, atonement for sin, and resurrection, God's grace and forgiveness.

But why did Morse tap out *that* message? Why was a word of gospel the first transmission over the wires? Just as it was unclear, even to Balaam on the mountain, whether he was going to bestow a blessing or a curse, it is unclear today whether the Internet is going to be a blessing or a curse. Surely man, in his Promethean science and technology, "hath wrought" the Internet. But what hath God wrought?

If the Internet is a tool, it can be used for the service of God and our neighbor. Even though the Internet is, on one level, the creation of man, it is still part of the world the Lord created and instructed us to care for. A PC lets people write, make music, crunch numbers, and do a thousand other tasks. It lets people do things easier or perform tasks that were expensive or impossible before. It can be a design studio, printing press, or virtual accountant. The importance of technology is not to be taken lightly just because it is not directly spiritual. All of life belongs to God. And so does technology.

CHAPTER THREE

Networking:
The Community Technology

§

A t first—and even when they had sprung up on desktops everywhere—computers were just major appliances. Very geeky major appliances. They were a great way to process words, crunch numbers, play games, and be more productive. But then they began to talk to each other. And soon not only computers but also human beings found themselves wired together.

The major cultural impact of computers came when they became a communications medium. They enabled individuals to connect with each other, with no restrictions of space or distance, linking people together into communities that had nothing to do with a sense of place.

The Internet creates a public space where one never existed before. While television closed many doors to interpersonal relations, the Net found new ones to open. The person one meets might be in St. Louis or Estonia.

Millions have close acquaintances whose only connection is Internet account to Internet account. In the real world they would never have come together; yet their interests tie them via E-mail, chat room, or mailing list.

People are meeting each other and getting married over the Internet. Instead of meeting in bars, people go on the Net and meet by typing at one another. Then, maybe, the two can agree to meet in the flesh.

Online relationships are an example of the oddity of virtual meetings. People get ideas of one another based solely on exchanged words. This means different parts of their personalities are revealed at first. Then people try the waters on the phone, seeing if the other person is for real. Then the time comes for a "facemeet." This often means driving or flying to see someone they think they know all about but have never met. Sometimes it works, but often it doesn't. Often people experience heartbreak when reality demolishes their fantasy, though sometimes future husbands and wives do find each other in this way.

From love to business, people find each other. This challenges the idea that technology is depersonalizing, taking away people's personalities and humanity, replacing it all with an iron, efficient conformity. Elderly people in nursing homes are overcoming their isolation and loneliness by keeping in touch with far-flung family members and getting to know new people online. People with idiosyncratic or highly specialized interests—from Patsy Cline fans to aficionados of nineteenth-century Napoleonic naval battles—can find kindred spirits on the Web.

Not all online talk is as brain-dead as some think the stereotype indicates. These so-called virtual communities of the like-minded can engage in spirited debates or high-toned intellectualized discourse or pursue trivial pursuits with passionate intensity, all in their little circles of like-minded screennames, which may include participants from all over the world. Following such discussions can provide an education in subjects no college could ever teach. There's an expert on anything lurking somewhere in a discussion group, ready to answer any question.

Sometimes the communal possibilities of the Internet have wider social and political ramifications. A motto of the Internet is that information wants to be free. Ideas, experiences, facts, and arguments can flow freely, from person to person, at nearly the speed of light. This includes political and politically charged information, not often let out by the big companies that own printing presses and TV stations. The Internet is an alternative media, one that is not one-way, from the top down, but rather interactive, one in which everyone with a computer can contribute and have a say.

One reason people have been able to keep talking so long— and about so many things, both good and bad—is that Internet services don't care what people say and by law are not responsible for what someone types. This became final in May 2000 when the Supreme Court let stand a lower court ruling that such providers aren't responsible when a user defames someone using their services. The case that tested this involved a Bronxville, New York, teenager named Alexander Lunney. He had opened a Prodigy account under his name back in 1994, and an impostor sent out a nasty E-mail in Lunney's name to a local Boy Scout leader, who then contacted the police. The company told the boy his account was being closed, then apologized when they learned of the impostor's role, nevertheless closing additional accounts under variations of Lunney's name. Lunney's father sued Prodigy (*Lunney v. Prodigy Services*) for negligently allowing accounts to be opened by someone else in his son's name and for defamation of character and emotional distress. The New York Court of Appeals ruled that Prodigy— and all the other service providers—are not responsible for the contents of E-mail or bulletin board postings, being no different from a phone company or telegraph operator.[1]

That decision effectively keeps E-mail providers out of customers' messages. Only when someone violates the service agreements will they take action, and even then they are often slow. Since online services are not considered the publishers of the messages, they can't be sued for their contents. Given that they don't have any right to censor, they must allow anything and everything to pass in and out.

The communal nature of the Internet makes it a potent social force. Where else can one be alone in a room and still be lost in conversation? To be sure, this is not always a good thing, providing new means of escapism and the substitution of phony identities and relationships for the real thing. Nevertheless, today just checking one's E-mail has become an important part of people's everyday routine. It consumes an increasingly large portion of the day and an increasingly large portion of people's intellectual and emotional energy. This is how it happened.

BUILDING THE NET

The Internet itself developed on a different track from the PC. For years the medium was trapped within the confines of mainframes. Only recently has it become a mass medium. When it was started, nobody thought it would become a way to get a job, make money, find free stuff, and do matchmaking. People then were more concerned about surviving the Cold War with the Soviets.

On September 2, 1969, in a research lab at the University of California-Los Angeles, two unwieldy computers were connected by a mere fifteen-foot cable. After some twiddling and fiddling, they started passing test data back and forth to one another. Like Samuel Morse communicating from Baltimore to

Washington, "what hath God wrought" and like Alexander Graham Bell telephoning Watson in the next room, this exchange of bits gave birth to the Internet.[2]

The plans for such a system date back to 1957, when the Defense Department got worried about the Soviet Sputnik satellite launch. They needed a decentralized, fast, and efficient way for research computers around the world to talk about it. They were also looking for ways to create a computer network that would survive a nuclear war, in case the Cold War got hot.

In 1961 Len Kleinrock, a graduate student at MIT, wrote a paper about the feasibility of linking computers and offering suggestions about how it might be done. He became a professor at UCLA in 1963. It was Professor Kleinrock who flipped the magic switch that day in September 1969. That year the Department of Defense Advanced Research Projects Agency (ARPA) linked four universities in ARPANET, an ancestor of today's Internet. A year later ten universities were online, using similar protocols used today by chatters, Web surfers, and downloaders.

But this was by no means the Internet we know now. It was a cold, dark, user-unfriendly place, controlled by a high priesthood of research geeks. Access was permitted only to the few who could get a security clearance for a user name and password. It was a government project and a military project, but since it was for scientists, universities naturally got involved.

The universities, in turn, went on to set up their own separate networks, as did various businesses. When these private networks hooked into the government's ARPANET, the result was the Internet. Before long the online elite multiplied and started talking to one another about less arcane topics than nuclear secrets and engineering data, passing around office jokes, software tips, and *Star Trek* trivia. More and more people got into the act. When the Internet broke away from the government and became an unregulated public commodity, such is the magic of free enterprise economics that it became fruitful and multiplied.

THE ELECTRONIC BULLETIN BOARD

Ordinary people couldn't start talking online back in 1969. After all, the Internet itself was all but inaccessible until the mid-1990s. Yet hobbyists starting in the late 1970s started connecting their computers and getting to know one another.

Way back in 1978, Ward Christensen and Randy Seuss lit a fuse that would take two decades to explode. With their primitive computers and a little programming, the two built the world's first computer bulletin board. Named simply CBBS, for Computer Bulletin Board System, it was a system that let people on home computers talk and exchange data via their modems, over telephone lines.

For the first time a home computer was a communications device. The ramifications are obvious now, but until the 1990s the Internet was still basically a research tool. People got their entertainment and news from the TV and communicated with each other over the telephone or by writing letters. The computer's capacity to merge all of these media was nowhere in sight. Not even people who were online in the early 1990s saw it coming. But just as some of our ancestors used smoke signals to talk to one another, so these early cyberspace pioneers hooked up their Apples and Commodore 64s to a new world of communication.

In those early days few people thought of getting online. For a few years CBBS was a rare bird. But then a flood of home computers came from IBM, Commodore, Atari, and others, and people discovered new things they could do with them. People started buying 300- or 2400-baud modems and launching their own boards. Grown-ups and crafty teenagers mingled together talking, playing games, and passing around software. A subculture of hackers and pirates grew up on the boards, passing around computer games and thinking up mischief.

This was a far cry from surfing the Internet. This was BBSing, firing up your modem to direct-dial another board that was usually hosted by another hobbyist in your town. Each city, with its local telephone numbers, had its own boards. Usually there was just one phone line; so people had to wait for someone else to get off the system before they could get on. Once they managed to log in, users often faced a time limit of fifteen minutes to an hour. Those who donated money or helped out often got extra time. But there usually were not all that many people on a given bulletin board. And reading and answering what other people had posted had to be done one caller at a time.

Until the Internet went pop in the mid-1990s, this world was what thousands knew as cyberspace. A person might spend hours hopping from board to board seeing what was new. Since one or more private citizens controlled each board, they kept absolute control over their systems. Privacy was nonexistent. E-mail and discussion groups were often screened or censored to prevent problems.

Different boards, as would happen with web sites, went in different directions. Mega-huge BBSes often had several phone lines and made subscribers pay for access. Other smaller lists tried to serve specific clientele. Early stabs at Christian community began here, and long-standing theological discussions and prayer circles started up. Hackers and punk teenagers hung out on their boards, trading the latest pirated games for Commodore 64 and trying to figure out how to crack the phone system. Unlike the Internet, people on different boards often didn't know of one another. Each group was a separate entity unto itself.

This was a tinkerer's domain; so boards went up and down overnight. People passed around lists of bulletin boards that quickly became obsolete. Different boards became like social clubs and watering holes for different groups to hang out. The groups sometimes became very close-knit. Since people usually lived in the same town, online friends could meet at a local pizza parlor and see those to whom they were typing.

Some boards tried to hook up to one another in large regional or international networks like Fidonet or RelayNet. These networks became bureaucratic nightmares, since communication involved crossing numerous PCs owned by private volunteers. Long-distance calls in the middle of the night powered the system, and sometimes mail took days to get through. Since the phone bills were often high and the tools to route messages were complicated, disputes often broke out within these networks.

A better, though less personalized, solution to nationwide communication came with the development of commercial online services like GEnie, CompuServe, or The Source. These were self-contained worlds that connected people the way America Online does today, except without an outside line to the Net. Each company posted features they thought would be of interest to their subscribers. These included news postings, access to various publications, games, and so on. They were big bulletin boards that could include little bulletin boards to which subscribers could contribute and send E-mail to each other (to other subscribers, that is, not to anyone on some other self-contained service). CompuServe, the one early online service that survived, became the most popular as users hit the forums and their early CB channels, the predecessor to the chat room. These online services charged per-hour usage fees, and the bills could shoot into hundreds of dollars per month.

A prototype of what would come was a site called the WELL. Founded as The Whole Earth 'Lectronic Link in April 1985 by techno-hippie Stewart Brand, it was an online companion to the retro-hippie magazine *Whole Earth Review*. It became a hangout for San Franciscans, techies, and Deadheads (Grateful Dead fans) and soon became a rare spot where average people could get on the government, defense department, research university network that would become the Internet. Unlike regular bulletin board sites, WELL promoted itself as more than a hobbyist hangout. It promised the ultimate in free speech, where participants could do or say anything they wanted.

In the early 1990s, the WELL was the hottest thing a civilian could get his hands on. There were smart people (who, alas, were almost uniformly leftist) talking and doing things on their computers. Who would have thought? Since the WELL's audience was closer demographically to that of many freelance writers, word of this place spread through the media in the early 1990s. The future to them was in "virtual community," which they thought looked like the coffeehouse crowd of the WELL.

USENET AND LISTS

In the meantime, the ARPANET—the linking of government and university computers—began developing a life of its own. Not only defense specialists and research scientists but your average college student could access it. Then there was the WELL crowd. Soon more and more people were using it, and for less and less weighty reasons than it was designed for.

Before the advent of the World Wide Web, with its full-color visuals and easy-click icons, the Internet was not a user-friendly place. Cyberspace then was an obscure realm of texts and funny instructions. It usually lived on a nerdy operating system called UNIX, not a nice graphical interface like what runs Macs and Windows. Access was locked away to the few and technological. No one back then would have dreamed that commercial Internet services would be falling all over one other trying to help people get online. Many saw it as the fiefdom of the lucky few, to be kept from the masses. Getting help was often difficult and frustrating.

But it did have E-mail. And something called Usenet, which was the coolest thing on the Net before the Web came around. This was a collection of newsgroups, or discussion groups, that let people talk to one another on different topics. These have long names connected by periods, like rec.arts.movies.reviews or alt.music.beach-boys or sci.physics.computational.fluid-dynamics. The convention became its own joke, producing things like alt.swedish.chef.bork.bork.bork, alt.barney.dinosaur.die.die.die or alt.buddha.short.fat.guy.

Usenet was the first major cultural phenomenon of the Net. Born way back in 1979, it became the greatest hub of activity seen to date. Occasionally visited by WELL members and lucky BBS users who could score a university connection into the fledgling Internet, the newsgroups showed that a large population wanted to use the medium for something besides programming and surviving a nuclear war. Enough people were in the newsgroups, even in the late 1980s, for serious discussions of antiques or opera or British horror movies. (Sadly, this is also the place where the cyber-porn craze started. The various alt.sex groups had dot categories for nearly every fetish, with people posting pornography for global distribution.)

Usenet is the source of familiar standards and conventions that survive today. Online fights became like a sport and picked up the term "flame war." Someone joked that junk mail posts were "spam," and the name stuck. A novice user became known as a "newbie," and a message intended to fool somebody was called a "troll." The stage was set.

Perhaps Usenet's greatest gift was the FAQ, or Frequently Asked Questions, list. Since a new group of college students got E-mail accounts every September and would be clamoring to sign onto the lists of their choice, newsgroup readers started posting these lists about topics from the Civil War to cryptography, explaining the basics about a topic and the parameters of each group. It was a rare chance when the old Internet reached out to help new users, if only to shut up annoying questioners.

Usenet had one critical factor that helped both its rise and downfall: It was completely unmoderated. Anyone could post, and anyone with an account could receive messages. Since the only gate to entry was Internet access, the groups reflected their academic roots—intelligent, but often ornery and countercultural. A group could be invaded by its ideological enemies or other harassers, resulting in flame wars. Christians, satanists, and atheists invaded each other's groups, for example, making a nuisance of each other.

While Usenet was growing, some users started using E-mail to develop discussions in a less public arena. Meanwhile, academic servers started giving space to mailing lists, where people could hold discussions of scholarly topics. A group of people joins, and a message sent to the list is sent to everyone by the main computer. Replies get passed around, and discussion can go on for years. These resembled BBS discussion areas and newsgroups, but they were a bit more focused and intimate.

These groups started out as glorified academic journals, but they expanded to cover every possible topic. Groups of friends would build invitation-only lists that resembled the camaraderie on some BBSes.

On Usenet, people could come and go as they pleased or say whatever they liked. On BBSes, discussions were limited to a geographic area and could vanish with the board. The list-servers offered a more stable, intimate environment. Lists can keep the same regulars for months or years. Newcomers to the Net don't need any special software to join or read. For religious discussions, this is ideal because one can keep discussions to a specific subject without worrying about invasions from wandering kooks who show up to cause trouble.

Lists come in two shapes—direct and digest. A list member can get all his messages as they come in or get them in one big pile at the end of the day. Thus the list can play to two types of participants. One, the poster, can contribute, talk, argue, and ask questions. The lurker can sit back and watch as if it were a TV show or unfolding chapters in a book. Moderators were often present, working to keep conversation on topic, introduce new members, and enforce the group's self-chosen rules. When a list must close, former members often will start a new group reuniting the old gang.

These discussion areas are more than just forums for sending memos or even a return of the art of letter writing. This new electronic correspondence amounts to a brand-new form of writing. It is part postcard, part phone call, part debate. Internet posts have the semipermanence and premeditation of writing, yet the immediacy of interpersonal communication.

Writing can be far more expressive and thoughtful than face-to-face conversation, since there are no social contexts—no shyness or stage fright, no person-to-person niceties to get in the way, no need to talk off the top of one's head to keep the conversation going—only the expression of what is on one's mind. Writing that is too detached from an audience can become an impersonal, formal, turgid discourse into a void. Electronic correspondence is spontaneous and relational, like speech, while still being a self-contained, self-controlled expression. Thus, a patina of intimacy hangs over online conversations that are seldom found in either other written texts or face-to-face conversations.

Not that this is always a good thing. Electronic correspondence—whether in the guise of E-mail, list posts, or chats—tends to be highly informal, casual, and slangy. Because writing on the Internet is so spontaneous, it can become unorganized and incoherent, mere babbling if it goes on for long. Fortunately or unfortunately, it usually doesn't. Posts tend to be short, but that means that ideas can seldom be explored in detail or in depth. Electronic writing is no substitute for the more sustained discourse of books. But at its best, it can approximate the Socratic dialectic of questions and response, the back-and-forth discussion that classical educators have always hailed as the best way of attaining personal understanding.

This odd hybrid of writing and speech began to develop stylistic conventions of its own. These joined in the emerging customs—which all cultures sooner or later devise—that goes under the umbrella of "netiquette." People realized that interpersonal relationships were building without any clue of location, clothing, age, or gestures. The social cues given in speech and face-to-face conversation—such as the tone of voice to indicate a joke or sarcasm—began to be compensated for by "emoticons," the little smiley or winking faces made by keyboard strokes, symbols that can be as annoying as they are necessary. The famous sideways smiley face began popping up to tell people not to take someone's comments too harshly. Typing in all capitals was frowned upon, because it looks like someone is shouting. In addition, acronyms like ROTFL (rolling on the floor laughing), AFAIK (as far as I know) and IMHO (in my humble opinion) popped up to save typing and as expressions of humility or a specific response. Such conventions are conversational, yet they cannot be pronounced and can only be typed and silently read.

Internet groups themselves became somewhat less freewheeling and more disciplined. Many became stricter about posting on-topic, and members who posted unnecessary material were encouraged to take it elsewhere. All in all, despite the flame wars a modest spirit was encouraged. In various areas of cyberspace, people leaned toward the two commandments of the Fidonet BBS Network: "Thou shalt not excessively annoy others" and "Thou shalt not be too easily annoyed."

Eventually word spread about the Net outside the engineering departments and computer science labs. Humanities and other departments of various universities also wanted to send E-mail, exchange files, and hit Usenet. By the mid-1990s, it became commonplace for universities to give Internet access to undergraduates. Then premium online services like Delphi and America Online offered portals onto the Net. These were no longer self-contained mega-bulletin boards but "onramps onto the information superhighway." Everything and everyone became connected to each other. The Net was opened up to the masses.

ENTER THE SPAM

In the months before the Web took things by storm, Usenet was still the great town square, but it was already suffering from a population explosion. Veterans complained of a "permanent September," referring to the academic calendar, meaning endless new users were appearing who were uncivilized to cyberculture.

The presence of too many newbies broke down the long-time relationships that had been established within groups. The intimate personal relationships, even between those who would flame each other, were further challenged when less personal and more commercial interests invaded the forum. Many long-time users were unprepared with what happened next—a spam explosion.

One of the world's great annoyances launched into infamy on April 13, 1994. Immigration lawyers Laurence Canter and Martha Siegel sent a stream of ads to countless Internet discussion groups. They offered their services to help foreign students get their green cards. With this first major online junk mail campaign, spam was born.

Canter and Siegel are forgotten today, but the "Green Card Lawyers" were the most hated people in cyberspace just a few years ago. They soon published an awful book, *How to Make a Fortune on the Information Superhighway*, singing the joys of unsolicited solicitation.

Endless copycats followed, pitching everything from pornography to get-rich-quick schemes to mail-order ham. Soon anyone who put their E-mail address out in public, from a chat room to a web site, got pelted with useless junk. The reaction has been a desperate search for a way to stop the flow. So far everything from E-mail filters to lawsuits have been tried, but the flow hasn't ebbed.

Junk mail first invaded newsgroups, then E-mail as shady characters discovered that if they sent enough messages, somebody would respond. Since E-mail could be mass-produced and mass-distributed, advertisers, scam artists, psychotics, and the emotionally needy exploited it. It also became an advertising vehicle of choice for pornographers. Formerly one had to actively search out pornography on the web. Now it searches out you.

Since junk mailers spend almost nothing to send a message,

they can send to millions of accounts. If only a tiny percentage responds—1 percent of a million is 10,000—they will make money. Mainstream marketers do everything possible not to be connected with spam, usually by making customers give permission to be sent ads in E-mail.

The spammers themselves hide behind a veil of phony return addresses and bizarre bulk mailing software. If they lose one E-mail account, they can simply jump to another one somewhere in the world—outside the jurisdiction of any laws against them—and start again. And the volume of spam makes finding every culprit too time-consuming. Even federal investigators can only chase so many bad guys. And often spammers are not technically frauds but merely use extremely sleazy marketing tactics. After all, somebody buys the stuff those guys sell. Thus junk E-mail and crack cocaine have something in common: Everybody hates them, yet they are too profitable to be driven from society.

DEEP IN THE MUD

With all of the newbies, the spam, and the commercialism of the Internet, many longtime posters started bailing out, and many groups turned to chaos and fell apart. By then (about 1995) the Web had been invented and was drawing people away. Usenet survived, but its growth was stunted. It still exists and carries on as a backburner element of the Net, a legacy of the old days.

Another part of the Net whose growth was stunted by the Web but had been an important part of the online culture was the world of MUDs. Multi-User Dungeons are complex, labyrinthine role-playing games in which people become characters in an online fantasy. While there, people can make online friendships with other people in the game.

Instead of being immersed in 3-D graphics, early users wandered around in a text-based adventure that was harder to play and required more imagination than later computer games that had the advantage of sophisticated visuals. MUDs became famous with social scientists and a few enterprising journalists because players could take up alter egos and live like them as if characters' relationships were real life.

This led some to speculate that the Internet would become a tool for people to adopt any identity, gender, or personality interchangeably. Netizens would thus live in "virtual community," following their bliss with any identity they wanted.

For some, these online role-playing games were quite addicting. Others found that the text-based, command-heavy experience wasn't pleasant. Most people decided that they liked their birth characteristics and actual identities after all. The masquerade became restricted to places like games and chat rooms. Many new users who visited MUDs had run-ins with old-timers who resented anyone moving in on their turf. So users took to the Web for gaming and used the simpler chat-room format for conversations.

Once the Web took off (the tale to be told in the next chapter), non-Internet connections became obsolete. Most online services shifted to the Net, with CompuServe and America Online surviving (and later merging) as hybrids between the old and new. Both offered their self-contained features—functioning like the old bulletin boards, only with sophisticated graphics—while also becoming Internet Service Providers (ISPs). AOL found great success as an online bunny slope, an easy way for the non-technical and the uninitiated to get in on the Internet. BBSes died off en masse as people left their isolation for more wide-open spaces. The WELL survived, changing owners several times, and was eventually absorbed into Salon Magazine.

The old ideas of community come back often in new forms. Sony took the old multilevel dungeon idea and developed a game called EverQuest, charging players $9.89 to live in a 3-D fantasy world. Users can control eight characters that interact, trade, fight, marry, and coexist with other players. Unlike typical role-playing games, death isn't forever, just a temporary setback. EverQuest follows in the footsteps of MUDs, letting people take up alter egos. But this time developers knew there was money to be made serving those who do want an escape, especially if they are willing to pay for their addiction.

The level of commitment to such games grew beyond anyone's imagination. Starting out as actors in an improvised play, role-players can become like citizens of an ethereal kingdom as the characters get more powerful and amass treasure. Those who don't want to wait have found they can often find goodies like armor or swords or a really nice cloak by buying them—for real money—from other players. Thousands of dollars can be spent on expensive items that only exist on a computer screen, like a Tunare executioner's hood or a lovely Tribunal bat skull earring.[3]

Why would someone buy imaginary swords and sorcery paraphernalia? Part of the reason is that some players see the game as an alternate existence preferable to the real world. Part of it is that these games are so expansive and complicated that getting a powerful character could take weeks. Some players can spend over forty hours a week just playing a game!

LIVING ONLINE

Most people on the Internet don't want to take up an alternate lifestyle. They just want to get work done or find what interests their tastes. So when Netscape made the Web browser popular, allowing the masses to find what was out there, the rush was on. As one observer noted, it was like a parade breaking out in a bomb shelter. This "cyberspace" stuff became more and more attractive. People started directing their lives toward their E-mail accounts. They began making more and more business deals, started love affairs, and even committed crimes with their mice and modems.

They began living in a realm without location, existing only as electronic bits and bytes spread over millions of computers— a non-place that holds thousands of "sites" and communities. The Net is like television. It doesn't become one's life, and yet it moves into a more and more central role. A person can easily use all available free time surfing away.

There are two types of people on the Net—hunters and gatherers. Hunters want to find something, to get the latest new thing. They'll dig around, finding information and goodies and bringing them home to their hard drives. The Internet is a place to go for these people. Others are gatherers, who see the Net as a necessity but not a treasure chest to be mined. They go online, get their E-mail, grab a few news headlines and stock quotes, and then go do something else. Both use the Internet as a tool, but they approach it in different ways. Gatherers are a big hit with Internet services since they do their online business quickly and use few resources on their unlimited access accounts.

People who spend too much time on the Net can face some kind of trouble. Every college has horror stories about students who killed their grades by too much surfing. Companies that give accounts to their workers have to be wary of the extended coffee breaks they take while doing personal E-mail at the desk. Pop psychologists talk about curing "Internet addiction." "Internet widows" are neck and neck with "football widows" in the ranks of harried wives.

The Internet offers the best and worst of human culture side by side. Online casinos, for example, have quietly attracted millions to the fun of having their wallets drained by gambling without leaving their own chairs. Players say online gaming spares them the time, expense, and discomfort of Las Vegas and Atlantic City. The downside is that someone who gambles on his computer never really leaves the casino. Someone who flies into Vegas will lose money and go home, while an online gambler can keep trying and trying.

In the mid-1990s, thinkers such as would-be futurist Howard Rheingold prophesied an era of "virtual community," where the masses would find meaningful relationships that transcended race, gender, age, or ethnicity. Others took the MUDs and chat rooms as evidence that people would live with artificial personal and sexual identities in new lives in cyberspace. Neither happened.

What does occur today is that people naturally segregate themselves according to their interests. They may spend a few minutes flipping around web pages or months debating on a mailing list. Many people don't have the time or inclination to do that kind of digging, so they simply use E-mail and the basic features offered by their Internet provider.

Newsgroups and mailing lists have survived, while a new breed of Web-based bulletin boards is popping up everywhere. Those who interact today are interested in a specific topic, which may be horribly mundane. It isn't community in the big-picture sense, but rather the camaraderie one might find at a social club or cocktail party.

Often "community" is just people posting responses to a news article on the Web. A few commercial web sites offer free services that will construct mailing lists for people who want to form communities of their own (in exchange for tagging ads in messages). This has led to a proliferation of interest groups and online communities that anyone can join and form. Chat rooms live on in many ways, though they tend to get more signal than noise.

All this virtual life may be creating a world of loners, at least according to a controversial Stanford University study that claimed in early 2000 that the Internet keeps people away from friends, family, offices, stores, and even television. Computers by nature isolate people. A whole family may stare into the glow of a normal TV, but rarely a computer monitor. The survey from the Stanford Institute for the Quantitative Study of Society noted that people use the Internet more as their experience with it grows; the more they use it, the more they want to use it.[4]

One-fourth of regular Net surfers said their use "has reduced their time with friends and family, or attending events outside the home," according to the Stanford report.[5] The same number say they do more work at home instead of at the office. TV viewing was down for 60 percent, and newspaper reading was down for one-third of Internet regulars.

This raises some important questions about how the Net is changing, if not depleting, our social worlds. What happens when most people spend most of their vital hours staring at a screen and punching buttons? What becomes of community, place, hearth, home, and other elements of physical society? Technology can bring some people together, but it can rip others apart.

But what the Internet has done, for better or for worse, is bring together people who wouldn't be together otherwise.

CHAPTER FOUR

The Weaving of the Web: The Realm of the Hyperlink

§

The computer was one piece of the puzzle. Then came the Internet, as computers and people became wired together. But there was one more development that has made possible the total information environment that we live in today—the World Wide Web.

The technology that has spun the Web is the capstone to the new medium, the missing link that suddenly makes it possible for all of the century's media innovations—the computer, the television, the telephone, fiber optics—to come together into one entity whose whole is greater than the sum of its parts. No longer is the Internet just text, an assembly of typed words, marvelous as that may be. With the Web, the Internet becomes visual, something to see, something to move around in; it conveys the illusion of space, of cyberspace.

The Web also makes the wonders of the information universe accessible to everyone. You do not have to be a techie or a UNIX master or a student of computer ways to use the Internet. You only have to click a mouse. With the Web you can actually find things on the Internet. The information is not only out there somewhere; it is accessible. This puts some powerful tools in the hands of ordinary folks. Now nearly anyone can not only visit but construct virtual malls that can sell things and make money but that occupy no land and require no buildings. Small businesses, interest groups, and individuals can not only have their own web sites, they can make use of everyone else's. The power to have a presence on the Web is available to just about anyone, at almost no cost.

Scientists working on the Human Genome Project—mapping the DNA that constitutes the human genetic code—are putting their findings on the Web. The data on a single chromosome would take up the equivalent of 949 newspaper pages. When the first chromosome was mapped and the findings published in the scientific journal *Nature*, there was not room enough in the journal to print the full code. No matter. The bewildering sequence of chemical symbols—A's, C's, G's, and T's—is all posted on the Web, for the scientists who can make use of it. (It's at www.genome.ou.edu.)[1]

When Pathfinder landed on Mars on Independence Day in 1997, NASA put out the data, and photographs were received in real time over the Web. The site scored a record 33 million hits a day as people clicked on to witness directly, in their own homes, the sights from the surface of another planet.

The wonders of the Web, what it makes possible, are occasions for praise. That there are spiders in the Web—corruption and temptations—goes without saying. But one can only appreciate how finely it is woven.

DIGITAL PICTURES AND CLICKABLE HYPERTEXT

Toiling away at a particle physics lab in Geneva, Switzerland, Tim Berners-Lee's interest in hypertext turned into the revolution that turned the Net into a Web. He cooked up a scheme that let researchers combine ideas with the use of interlocking text, or hypertext. In 1989 he launched his project as a global experiment called the World Wide Web.

Hypertext is the key that made the Web different from an online filing cabinet or mailbox. The idea dates back to the 1940s, but Berners-Lee made the Internet clickable. A highlighted word, graphic, or other element on a web page can connect to any other element on any other page. Each webmaster controls his or her own sites, but everything hooks together. By clicking from page to page, it is possible to drill down to what one specifically wants.

Every element on the Web has a "universal resource locator" that lets another document point to it. By clicking on a headline, a news story pops up. Click on a company's name, and its home page will fire up. As a tool for digging around, it is unmatched.

Yet for a few years it was just another way to dig through text. Then a group of researchers decided to add pictures to the Web by designing a graphical browser. The NCSA (National Center for Supercomputing Applications), located at the University of Illinois, released Mosaic in February 1993, and the product was an instant smash. Mosaic soon mutated into a commercial software package called Netscape, and the boom was on. All the difficult commands required by the old text-based Internet melted away with the click of a mouse.

It was almost like when gold was discovered at Sutter's Mill or when silver was uncovered at the Comstock Lode, except that no one had to travel to mine this lode, and almost everything was free. Suddenly every conceivable company, group, and picture hit the Web, promoting both good and ill. Private individuals decided to be webmasters themselves and put their mark on the world by constructing home pages to display their interests to anyone who cared.

While some feared the world would drown in bomb-making secrets and pornography, others dreamed of the biggest thing since Gutenberg. Both were half right.

Unlike every other medium from books to shortwave radio, which are essentially self-contained, with the Web everything is interconnected (which is why it is called a web). Hypertext got hyper-fast. The Web grew exponentially. Millions of pages came up, and a site was available for anybody's budget. Services like Geocities and Xoom offered the masses a chance to devise sites of their own, while big corporate agencies and corporate technology departments cooked up titanic sites that cost millions.

Since then, nobody could keep track of the flood. To this day no one knows everything that can be found online. For the creative, no barriers can stop self-expression. Every kook and genius has a slot there. Every subculture that exists can find a home online where even a handful of cobelligerents can enjoy an outpost.

The Web means people can explore their interests in public, whether or not anybody's watching. A person can share his dreams, show off his wedding pictures, or write up his grievances against his boss. Bizarre cult followings can pop out of nowhere and attract huge responses, while most others fade into oblivion.

Though most noncommercial sites only get a smattering of attention, the Web has a flattening effect. Ugly web sites are just as downloadable as beautiful ones—and just as free. Bootleg *Playboy* pictures are as easy to find as Calvin's commentaries. The Web is the ultimate pluralism, the ultimate toleration, and the ultimate postmodernity.

In fact, the Web is the embodiment of postmodernity, in that all thoughts are reduced to the same level, all equally accessible and equally valid. If you don't like surfing up Calvinism, alternatives are available; a chaos cult, an atheist circle, or a radical Darwinist clique is easy to find. Nothing is holding you down or making you pay attention to anything in particular.

LIFE ON THE WEB

In the days before cable TV, people usually only had enough channels to count on one hand. The network news came on at dinnertime for everyone. America watched Frank Reynolds or Chet Huntley or Walter Cronkite because they had no choice. Now a home satellite system can offer hundreds of channels. But the Web is bottomless. If one could only find them, there are more interesting things online than one could possibly see.

Sometimes an unusual idea for the Web can have unusual consequences. David Felton's story started when he walked into his local Dunkin' Donuts store, ordered some coffee, and discovered he couldn't get any skim milk. So he complained openly on his web site, soliciting comments from others. Felton then spun off his complaining into a separate web site called www.dunkindonuts.org.

He ran it for two years. The twenty-five-year-old webmaster said people poured into the site, complaining about bad donuts and lousy service. In turn, company representatives visited the site every day, reading and responding to people who posted complaints. Eventually franchise owners jumped in, responding publicly about problems. The Dunkin' Donuts corporation didn't take the existence of a dunkindonuts.org lightly. The name was a sore point. So Felton was told to stop using their brand name. But the upstart decided to negotiate. He talked the chain into buying his site.[2]

Such a deal is an unusual way to manage public relations.

Since anyone can publish on the Net, anyone can rant and rave about brand names from Microsoft to K-Mart. In this case people griped about stale products, employees who can't speak English, and even donuts without filling. Normally such trivial concerns remained private, a bad experience that a consumer would keep to himself or a small circle of family and friends. But the Web magnifies things. Before the Internet, Felton's squabble with Dunkin' Donuts would have been impossible. Internet accounts pass out megaphones to the disgruntled.

Unlike TV watching, the Web is primarily a solitary medium. Who sits around the browser for a family evening of Yahoo? The very nature of the medium sets it apart as an individualist's medium. Each person gets to live in his or her own underground world, which allows for both self-expression and getting into trouble.

Men and women are both going online in vast numbers, for example, but they don't do the same things once they log in. A survey by research firm PC Data Online claims different genders go online with different mind-sets. Women are more likely to check their E-mail than men (81 percent versus 70 percent) and do research more often (52 percent versus 42 percent). The guys are twice as likely to download software and three times more likely to look up sports information on the Net. According to the poll of 1,479 males and 1,333 females, men are more likely to use the Net the way they do shopping: They get on looking for something specific. Guys often head for a search engine and hunt down their digital prey.[3]

Banner ads—those rectangular pitches placed on most commercial sites—are unpopular with both genders, but men are even less responsive than women. The poll reports that about half of women and only two-fifths of men click on them occasionally. Another one-third of women seldom do so. This is bad news for the many online media sites that rely on banners for their revenue. Since information wants to be free, the problem becomes how to pay for it. The model being attempted is that of network television, which funds its freely offered programming through advertising. TV commercials are proven to be effective; it remains to be seen if Internet advertisers are getting their money's worth. People generally watch commercials; not nearly as many people click the little boxes.

The gender gap extends to what people buy online. For example, greeting cards are the preferred purchases of 27 percent of women. Meanwhile, unfortunately, a big chunk of men—26 percent—say they prefer to buy pornography over the Net. The Internet doesn't make its users into new people. They carry their interests and attitudes onto the Internet and explore them. But those interests now have a wider scope, and the attitudes are magnified.

At any rate, the magic URL, the web address, has become ubiquitous. It beckons from stationery, E-mail, commercials, conversations, and cereal boxes. Once a novelty, web addresses have become as mundane as phone numbers.

The never-ending rush to "Click Here!" goes on and on. But though the Web keeps growing, the novelty is gone. People go onto the Web to do something, just as people get in their cars to go somewhere. Even bored office dwellers usually have a set of bookmarked distractions at the ready; so putting a new site in someone's face is difficult. Since every site is equally accessible regardless of content or quality, everyone competes with everyone else. Your pastor's sermons compete with the *New York Times*, Wal-Mart, and the Communist Party. Your pastor may not care about losing audience to some commercial site, but a store has to keep its products before as many eyes as possible.

WANT A COOKIE?

As the Web grew, webmasters looked for tools to help them track who comes and goes on their sites. Out of this was born a controversial tool known as the cookie, a term that doesn't refer to oatmeal or chocolate chip. A cookie is a tiny ID tag that many sites send to Web browsers. It means that the typical Net users give up a little bit of privacy when they surf the Net.

Cookies allow many web sites to greet you personally when you visit. Often they store passwords and personal information to save typing and make online shopping faster. Sites can use cookies to track where people go and what they do on their pages. Critics complain that they are being silently watched.

Cookies became controversial among hardcore Net users when they first became popular in 1996 and 1997. Many flipped an obscure switch in the preference settings of Netscape Navigator or Microsoft Internet Explorer that made their software refuse cookies or alert users before accepting them. A few people have developed software to make them go away.

Yet a quick trip to the cookies file in Netscape or the cookies directory in Internet Explorer gives a travelogue of where one has been online. The anonymity of the Web is an illusion. Parents and employees can see exactly what sites have been visited, just by checking the cookie directory. Those looking for a quick dose of paranoia might want to dig up these files and delete them. Often hundreds of sites have passed some form of ID code along.

Cookies represent the Great Web Trade-off—convenience for privacy. Even with Las Vegas-style security, a brick-and-mortar store can track what its customers buy, but it can't track where they browse. On the other hand, an online store can collect all sorts of data, in exchange for being able to hunt down an obscure item quickly and zap it to you overnight. Usually sites dumb down their own statistics to keep out of hot water over privacy and only keep records of aggregate customers instead of individuals.

Privacy groups and the industry are still haggling over standards on what can and can't be done with cookies. But cookies won't go away. Like it or not, companies collect data on where you've been on the Net and use it to help sell their products. The issue is like a real-life sci-fi novel, and we are only in the first chapter.

On the other hand, cookies are reminders that the Web is not as anonymous as people assume, which may be the first step to a semblance of social control, which the online world, like all cultures, desperately needs. In real life, a respectable citizen would feel ashamed to go into a strip club—someone might see him. Visiting a pornographic web site seems so anonymous that there are no social sanctions, no shame. But in fact someone may well be watching. Those contemplating visiting a particular site—such as responding to pornographic spam—would do well to consider whether or not they want there to be a record of this little visit. If not, they should think about what cookies are accumulating in their computer and stick with the sites they would not be embarrassed to have known.

THE GREAT E-COMMERCE BOOM

Through the 1990s, Web entrepreneurs grew tired of an industry focused on giving away stuff for free. So they cooked up a buzzword—*e-commerce*. Basically it means "make money online," usually by selling things. This was made easier by another technological/economic development, the cash-free, check-free way of spending money called the credit card. Consumers need only type in their number and the expiration date, then click on what they want. Coupled with the new one- or two-day delivering systems perfected by FedEx, UPS, and Post Office equivalents—themselves also largely made possible by computers with their bar-code tracking technology—shopping had never been easier. You could shop the wares of the world without leaving home and get it the next day. Soon giant catalog services popped up selling everything under the sun at the click of a mouse.

Naturally this sent some institutions into a panic—in particular, state and local governments dependent on sales tax revenue. They worried, quite rightly, that precious tax revenue from brick-and-mortar stores would be lost to slick online stores. Cyberspace exists in no locality. What jurisdiction does an online mall fall under? Who pays taxes when someone in California clicks onto an online music store whose owners live in Florida but whose warehouse is in Maine? Many state governors argue that customers who buy online from some other state should pay sales tax as if they were at a local store.

When online purchases cross state lines, customers usually pay no sales tax. That has some states complaining that residents are giving themselves a tax cut by buying online instead of at local businesses, even though the savings are often cancelled by the expense of paying postage and handling fees plus credit card interest (since web sites don't take cash).

Even though local stores survived the death of many downtown areas, endless generations of mail-order catalogs, direct mail, and even infomercials, somehow they think the Net will close the local strip mall.[4] Right now paying local sales tax is a nightmare even for Fortune 500 companies since there are literally thousands of jurisdictions whose rules must be followed. The fact is, many small businesses in tiny communities find that they can compete with the big boys by establishing a web site of their own and tapping into the vast market outside the city limits.

Some of the new online shopping emporiums seem counter-intuitive at first. For example, would you buy a used car from Bill Gates? Microsoft has a site called CarPoint that lets buyers go online for exactly the car they want, even the upholstery. Competitors like AutoNation and Autobytel are also shooting for this market, as are networks of local dealers. The winners on sites like these are auto buyers who have the knowledge and for-titude to jump back and forth among these sites to find exactly the car they want at the best price. The impersonality of the computer is a plus since it allows the buyer to dodge manipula-tive sales tactics. Consumers with the patience and know-how to do their own research can have more control over the price by using a variety of different web sites to learn exactly how much it costs dealers to put together the car they want. Armed with this information, they can go to dealers themselves and make them compete with each other to sell them their ideal car. Though consumers lose the ability to kick tires and go for a test drive, they come away with all the benefits of free market com-petition, even when they decide to just buy the car—armed with precious knowledge—at the local dealer.

Auto purchases may be the ultimate test for online shopping. Ford Escorts and Crown Victorias aren't like books and CDs that can be wrapped up and sent to a customer like traditional mail-order catalogs have always done. These are big-ticket items that usually require some physical contact with a local dealer—who, in effect, gets customers through these new middlemen—before making the deal. Even so, there are a few virtual dealerships, such as CarsDirect.com, that let the customer go all the way and buy online.

If someone can buy a Range Rover online, how about some-thing mundane like stamps? Could the Web shorten lines at the Post Office? Two startups, Estamp and Stamps.com, got permission from the U.S. Postal Service to offer Internet-based postage, proclaiming it the biggest thing since the first postal meter was invented eighty years before. The selling point is convenience, especially for small business and home offices that usually must lick stamps or hit meters.

E-commerce isn't just for well-heeled entrepreneurs dripping with investment capital. Online classifieds and auctions are all part of the same story. Anybody can join in—*anybody*. Take Arthur Shawcross, who sold kitschy paintings of Marilyn Monroe, stock-car driver Dale Earnhardt, and others on the auction site eBay. He was a little different from the usual seller: He was a convicted serial killer who had murdered eleven women in Rochester. When his prison keepers found out what he was up to, his computer privileges vanished in an instant.[5]

The Shawcross incident is one in a series of strange cases surrounding online auctions. These allow for pure free-market economics, with prices fixed merely by supply and demand. Anyone can offer something to sell online. People from around the world can bid on what they want, until buyer and seller agree on a price and the invisible hand of the marketplace records "sold." People will sell anything, it appears, including what is illegal. People have pitched babies, human kidneys, and even cocaine. Several fraud prosecutions have bubbled out of eBay among the thousands and thousands of legitimate auctions carried there. Perhaps the strangest legitimate (but halted) auction was posted by the shopping comparison site Priceman, which tried to auction nearly half of its equity for at least $10 million.[6]

Perhaps the reason why eBay and its competition get so much fervor and excitement is because the auction is a microcosm of the Internet itself. It is huge, flashy, and has seemingly everything. It is chaotic, libertarian, and totally laissez faire. It has good deals, bad deals, and deals that will summon the FBI.

Within the e-commerce world lurk numerous interlopers on the frontier. These are the ingenious operators who early on bought up the trademarks and generic names as Internet domains (those .com addresses) before the big corporations realized they needed to stake a claim on the Internet. A Virginia company called Network Solutions had a monopoly in the late 1990s and dished out domain names from McDonalds.com to AOL.com to Stamper.com on a first-come, first-serve basis. Those who lost out, who found that someone else had bought up their favored name, could either find another name or, in the case of a brand name that is a registered trademark, go to court.

Some of the early Web-savvy pioneers had the idea of registering popular names and corporation titles, then waiting for the Fortune 500 companies to pay hefty prices to buy them back. As time passed, these equivalents of the claim jumpers on the nineteenth-century frontier gained the name *cybersquatter.*

For example, Brenan Hofstadter registered the Internet domain names www.Wendys.org and www.WendysRestaurant.com and www.WendysRestaurants.com and WendysIntl-Inc.com, then tried to get the fast-food chain to buy the sites back from him. Wendy's International responded with a lawsuit, pointing out that he had played this game with other corporate brands belonging to the likes of Taco Bell, Coca-Cola, Sony Corporation, Subway restaurants, and Burger King.[7] Amazon.com was angry enough to file a RICO suit against the owners of "Amazon.gr, Greece's Biggest Bookstores," claiming the operators were running a "thinly veiled shakedown" attempt. The e-commerce giant claims the squatters tried to sell their company name back to them for over $1.6 million. Like Wendy's, Amazon.com refused to pay and claimed the interlopers were threatening their company's reputation. In February 1999 Microsoft got a judge to force two Houston men to turn over eleven Internet domain names to Microsoft, including microsoftwindows.com and microsoftoffice.com. Eventually the law will catch up with the new technology, once it figures out what is going on.

When the dust settles, a new breed of retailers will rise from the pile of wild ideas and madcap competition. Ultimately online purchasing will coexist beside catalogs, direct mail, regular stores, and everything else. At its most vibrant, e-commerce takes the wild diversity of the Web and applies it to products that can be downloaded, delivered, or shipped via UPS or some other service.

Among the Turkish bazaar of products and wild bursts of personal creativity is the so-called new media—either original content produced straight to the Web or something from somewhere else (like TV, newspapers, or books) repackaged into hypertext. For those who don't like the expense of ink, paper, and postage, the Web is like a vast library, publishing house, and entertainment studio all in one, all accessible on one's desktop and all virtually for free.

PLAY THAT DIGITAL MUSIC

Music online was a rather quiet field, except for selling albums, until a file format called MP3 popped up and created some of the hottest controversy on the Net. This was an unintended consequence of the software industry, rather than the consciously pursued technologies that gave us breakout formats like compact discs and DVD. MP3 was created as just another way to compress multimedia, so that data does not take up so much space on a file.

But what it did was to make it feasible for music to be passed back and forth on the Internet. MP3 allows CD-quality music to take up less disk space, so music can be downloaded without filling up one's hard disk or overwhelming the storage device on a disk drive. A song stored in MP3 format usually takes about a megabyte per minute of songs, well within the capacity of contemporary computers and their disks. Store MP3s on a CD-ROM and you can get about ten hours on one disk.

Once MP3s hit the Internet, the term *MP3* replaced *sex* as the most-selected keyword on the major search engines. Suddenly people were scouring the Internet for free music. MP3 files are easily transferable, especially for those with high-speed connections like a cable modem or a university or work hookup. Since the files are relatively small, they are quickly transferable and can be posted to the Net or passed around easily.

Much of MP3's impact has to do with people who use it to bootleg their favorite albums and singles, to the chagrin of the record companies. Yet these files can open up a new world to a feisty upstart band. They can get their songs distributed right after being recorded, without having to deal with pressing CDs or the conventional channels of distribution. Bands are finding that a giveaway MP3 file can be a hook to sell a full-length CD, push a pay-download collection of MP3s, or promote a concert tour.

Getting noticed may be difficult. But with enough self-promotion there's always a chance. For those willing to do the work, MP3 and other digital formats decentralize the music business. Those who want to build a following have an open door.

This doesn't mean the major labels are going away; they still have the budgets, and they still have their extremely profitable music catalogs. The industry is working hard to develop technologies by which buyers can download music from label web sites, but for a fee. The impact may be more on production—no more need to manufacture little disks—and distribution, a threat to the record stores. Again, it is the middle man who is being bypassed. But this makes it easier for people who lack access to the record factories to play the same game.

At least here the little guy has a chance, even though it won't be easy. Getting ahead on the Net is a little like trying to be the most popular seashell on Venice Beach. Like anything else in new media, talent plus intestinal fortitude are prerequisites to success

Of course, MP3, like most innovations on the Internet, has its downside. Digital music suffers from its confinement to personal computers. One can buy portable players that connect to them, but they are expensive. A PC and a home stereo have different purposes, and they often stay in different rooms. Many users aren't interested in the hassle of finding unknown bands on the Net when they still have the FM radio and the usual CDs. And those who are stuck with slow modems at home will find downloading several megabytes for one song still too tedious.

So even though MP3 may have become bigger than sex on the Internet, the record companies aren't hurting much from the competition. What they are upset about is piracy, when people use their computers and Net connection to deprive them of royalties. This concern has helped squelch all sorts of other formats in the past, from double deck VCRs to digital audiotape.

A once-obscure piece of software called Napster turned the MP3 debate into a music industry panic. It let people collect directories of their favorite songs and trade them with thousands of others—directly off their hard drives.

This became a big hit on college campuses, and the Recording Industry Association of America has sued the developers, demanding $100,000 for each song traded. The San Mateo, California-based Napster Inc. argued that it wasn't responsible for others' actions. Various other tools can help people pass files around, but this program came under special attack because it was so easy to use.[8]

The record industry claimed that Napster and its equivalents are simply channels to pass around copyrighted materials without paying for them. Users claimed they aren't necessarily pirating or that trading songs on the Internet is a way of fighting back against a greedy cabal. The Napster debate was full of complaints about high CD prices, the dominance of a few record labels, and the unavailability of obscure or out-of-print music.

While lots of pirates use MP3, the format and its successors are a doorway into a world of possibilities. The underground created by MP3 has produced hordes of unsigned bands passing around songs on MP3. Sure, much of it is worthless—there is usually good reason why groups do not get signed—but some deserve and can now get attention.

BROWSING THE VIRTUAL SHELVES

One of the grand crusades of new media is making full-length books available, readable, and popular in digital form. The promise of the electronic book is all the text without the paper. The publishing industry still doesn't know what to do with the concept—and nobody knows how well people will take to reading on a screen. Yet the e-book has all the makings of a cultural revolution. You can have any material you want at a moment's notice, and hardly anything goes out of print.

Digital publishing lowers the barriers for people who want to spread their ideas to the world. From an e-mail passed to friends to a web site to an e-book, one can bypass the cost and hassle involved with pitching one's thoughts on paper. Since the entryway is easier across the board, the challenge becomes that of getting noticed in a sea of competitors.

Imagine that your personal library could be stored on a disk or on your hard drive. Paper books are heavy, are costly to ship, take up lots of space, and often break down with age. After all, a typical college student's textbook load can top 100 pounds. To move the bulk of such books to a more portable storage medium only makes sense.

At a press conference promoting the electronic distribution of one of his books, Michael Crichton said he loved the idea of cramming several volumes into a simple handheld device. "I take a suitcase (of books) with me on vacation because I'm not sure of what I want to read," he said.[9]

A rush of new technology is coming that will make print easier to read and more portable in electronic format. E-books are where the Internet itself was in 1994: Everybody knows something really cool is coming, but they don't know exactly what.

For those interested in putting Christian words into circulation, this is a great opportunity. It will not be necessary to please the publishing establishment that often ignores, avoids, or doesn't understand solid content. If general audiences accept e-books (and they will, in some fashion), then this opens a door to put material into their hands. The burden becomes that of attracting readers and recouping writers' investment in time and effort.

The rise of e-books will bring some of the energy and exuberance of the Net into the publishing world. If Christians take advantage of it, it can be a great force for cultural transformation.

Right now New York's and Nashville's publishing houses look at e-books both with excitement and fear. They'll have a new way to sell books, but they'll be working in a medium they don't understand. After all, ink and paper have done pretty well for a few centuries, and many publishers have long lineages. Thomas Nelson, for example, dates back to 1798.

So far the biggest splash in e-books was a publicity stunt by longtime best-selling horror writer Stephen King. He took the jump in the summer of 2000 with his grand experiment of offering a novel over the Net, one chapter at a time for only a buck an installment. Readers simply pay the money, download the file, and read it on their computers. One twist was an honor system, trusting that people would be ethical enough not to pass out copies to ten or twenty million of their closest friends. If not enough people sent in their dollars, he would simply stop writing. Since this experiment was from a master of suspense, readers by and large cooperated.[10]

To take a look at what can come from electronic publishing, just look on the Web. While best sellers and backlists may take a while to get posted online, plenty of material is already available for free.

A treasure trove called the Christian Classics Ethereal Library (http://www.ccel.org/) runs out of Calvin College. Harry Plantinga, an associate professor in the school's computer science department, maintains a collection of dozens of works from Thomas Aquinas to George Whitefield. His library includes gems like the traditional collection of the church fathers (all thirty-eight volumes), along with books from both the good guys and bad guys of Christian thought.

Plantinga says on the site that he's spent about an hour a day since 1993 building up his collection. His goal is to build a portable library that can be cheaply distributed on disk "to every minister, missionary, and seminary student in the third world who speaks English and has a CD-ROM drive."[11] He reports that in early 1999 the amount of traffic on his site was the equivalent of giving away a million books a year.

Other places have all sorts of works. If something is old enough to be in the public domain, it can be digitized and republished for free. Shakespeare's canon was converted long ago and is available from many sources or cheaply on CD-ROM. The University of Pennsylvania has a listing of online books (http://digital.library.upenn.edu/books/) that lists everything from Zane Grey's westerns to *McGuffey's Readers* to Karl Marx's communism—all available for easy download. It's like getting a college education at the touch of a button.

The first mover in this world of online publishing was a man named Michael Hart, who got access to the mainframes at the University of Illinois back in 1971. He realized that data could be endlessly replicated and passed around. Years before the Internet boom of the 1990s, he figured that the biggest value of all this technology was the ability to search and find library information. He started Project Gutenberg (http://www.gutenberg.net/) to convert and distribute public domain books. Today it puts out about a book a day, ranging from Dante to Arthur Conan Doyle.

So books are out there. All we need is the technology to make them readable. Electronic texts are typically used by people who want to search through them or find something they can't get elsewhere. But few print out *Hamlet* because cheap copies can be found at local bookstores, and reading on a screen is difficult for many.

Many people wonder if readers will agree to do leisure reading on an electronic screen. Some may download a chapter or two for a lark, but will they read the whole book on their computer? To get people to read e-books, the text has to come off the monitor in a convenient format. Printers are available, but they can be a pain to use, and pages can pile up. Who would print his own Bible?

Handheld electronic readers make reading off the screen a little more convenient. One wonders, however, if such devices will become the publishing equivalent of the microwave oven, which was billed as a revolution in cooking but is used in real life only for certain specific tasks like warming leftovers and making popcorn. With electronic books, every book is crammed into the same size format and similar fonts. The style and feel of a hardback or paperback is missing. But technology may solve even these problems.

For those who want digital distribution without the screen, a company called Sprout sells on-demand publishing, where a bookstore would have a special printer that would custom-make a volume for a customer within minutes of the order. This allows books to be published without the cost of a press run or the never-never land of being out of print. Readers still get the pleasure of holding a book, one that has been manufactured one at a time, just for them.

If handled well, this could help build a Christian cultural renaissance. Serious Christian work is underrepresented in the publishing industry as it exists today. Electronic publishing opens the door to independents who can take advantage of the vacuum. The challenge becomes marketing, getting people to know the product is out there.

Books can now be written without fear that unsold self-published books will just pile up the garage. Reams and reams of hard-to-find material can be brought back into print indefinitely. If one wants to fight a culture war, so to speak, this is a way to store up ammunition.

If the Web has become a great Mars Hill of people promoting every idea imaginable, so will electronic publishing. There is much material that deserves to be republished and written. If Christians leave the publishing world of the future as just a continuation of what exists today, they will have lost a great opportunity.

Electronic publishing gives anyone a press. The competition

for attention will be fierce. The book world will converge with the Web world. When the dust settles, what remains may not be one industry dominated by a handful of Manhattan-based monoliths but a true marketplace of ideas.

Technology isn't making reading go away. It simply changes how we read and where we get it all. Electronic books pose a whole new way to create and find reading material. Once the traditional gatekeepers relax control of their industry, that will create an incredible challenge and opportunity for Christians.

ALL THE NEWS THAT'S FIT TO UPLOAD

Even though electronic books boast great potential, online news is the most famous, most discussed category in new media. Your local newspaper doesn't want to be buried by the Internet, which is why most papers are freely accessible on the Web, even though few receive much return on the investment. For five years papers have jumped into hypertext, giving people a newsstand covering every spot on the planet. And with so many competitors, publishers are scratching their heads about how to attract advertisers.

Newspapers hate the idea of giving content away. Many publishers dream of being able to collect "micropayments" of a penny or two per article. Right now the economics of online news means losing money, lots of it. But media outlets can't afford not to be online; so when the eventual weeding out of winners and losers comes, the news landscape may be radically changed.

Meanwhile, a host of original publications has popped up on the Web, from *APB Online* (crime) to *Wired News* (technology). While few dream of starting up a newspaper today with actual printing presses and rolls of newsprint, new online magazines have become the new way to deliver news. Some online magazines, such as *Slate*, tried to charge a subscription rate, but this went nowhere (though some must-read periodicals such as *The Wall Street Journal* have been able to charge readers who want to get it on the Web). Still, the online magazine *Salon* has started to get influential, breaking some news stories and making waves with their liberal political commentary.

Newspapers themselves are hurting with unoriginality. The old days of strong, sturdy papers with maverick publishers battling it out are almost forgotten. What we have now are bland rags that have a monopoly over their cities and lack both tone and drive. Also, with fewer papers around, rungs are cut off and opportunities closed for promising writers and editors to climb the ladder. Politically correct coverage and the oft-mentioned liberal bias are just part of the problem in a nation of dull print media. New media suffers from a bad reputation in some circles because of all the hype, hoaxes, and buffoonery that gets passed around online. Since there are no gatekeepers, discernment is a valuable instrument. Just as there are people who try to create havoc by trashing computers, so there are those who spread falsehood for fun and profit. This is most common in the financial world, where news and rumors ebb and flow, moving the investor's net worth along for the ride.

Online journalism has been held up as the harbinger of a new era, but right now the field is dominated by the Web versions of established titles. Lots of big news holes exist to be filled by feisty original content, but doing so is expensive, and media outlets often cough at the cost of running such an operation. If newspapers survived the phone, radio, and TV, they can survive the Internet. But will what's left be worth reading? Those opposed to liberal bias can now forge journalism of their own if they are willing to do what it takes to do so.

One form of content that seeks to be a form of digital wallpaper—in the background, yet omnipresent on users' computers—is the portal site. This would include the home pages of Yahoo.com, Lycos.com, and most Internet service providers. They are intended to be your starting point online, helping you go from there to find whatever you want. Portals usually include a search engine and Web directory, mixed in with regular features such as news clips and standardized links to often used services such as electronic travel agents and entertainment updates. These sites usually pay for the positioning, which, along with advertising, allows the portals to make money.

The portal strategy is that if people come to a single page every time they log in, the traffic will go through the roof. So many hits should attract lots of advertisers. Portals have become all the rage in everything from search engines to auto parts dealers. The strategy is to shove a bunch of features like free stock quotes and chat rooms into a site and hope it becomes "sticky" enough for users to make it their first stop when they log on. Portals also swap content with one another in order to "drive traffic" to themselves. The trouble is, portal sites are so repetitive, they all start looking alike. There is precious little reason to choose one over the other. But since a flood of new users is still washing into the Net, portal makers hope they can be at the right place at the right time to become someone's addiction.

A proposed alternative to the portal was something called "push" media, led by a product called Pointcast. Instead of loading up a browser, push products went on the Web while you were away and gobbled up news and information. It fed them either to a search engine or to the program's own menu system. The trouble with push technologies was that people didn't use them once the novelty wore off. They were intended to save download time by doing everything in advance, but users preferred to get their weather forecasts or news updates on their own. That all the extra downloading wreaked havoc on some office computer networks didn't help. Perhaps the idea was ahead of its time, but push lives on as an example that not every new idea for the Internet will succeed.

A more promising way of dealing with the conglomeration of information sites on the Web is the hypertext twist called the Weblog. A person goes out on the Web, finds what he sees is interesting, then links to all of it every day on his own page. It is like a popularized version of Matt Drudge's online stack of headlines from other news sources. The idea lets any user be his own editor, presenting the top stories that interest him. Other people may also be interested in what he said, so he can develop his own constituency. He, in effect, becomes their gatekeeper.

Webloggers are not normal journalists. Instead of writing news, they point to news. He or she searches the Web for cool links, usually interesting news sites, funny web pages, and new software. Then the favorites get put up on a web page that lists each link with a description of what makes it interesting. Thus a user comes back day after day to see interesting things.

Some can reach only a few dozen people a day; others reach thousands of readers on a daily basis. Such sites allow the owners to slice up the news, adding commentary as they see fit. People come to these sites because they reflect their personality; the weblogger's taste is close to that of the audience. Thus a thousand Dan Rathers bloom.[12]

With the demise of the establishment gatekeepers and the proliferation of information, people do need someone they trust to keep the gates. This is a role that Christians can rush in to fill, both for each other and possibly for outsiders who might be attracted to a well-designed, interesting set of suggestions and tips from Christians. Already Christian portals are being designed—which include features to sort out the bad stuff on the

Net—offering links of interest to Christians as well as original reviews, critiques, and features.

DO YOUR HOMEWORK

Just before the year 2000 came, the Internet's biggest crash was the *Encyclopedia Britannica*. The venerable reference guide decided to give away all thirty-two volumes and 44 million words on the Internet. When what used to cost $1,250 per set became available for free, the site was promptly deluged with users from around the world. The servers collapsed like Humpty Dumpty off a wall. Up went an apology for the "temporary slowdown" and a promise that the new site would be back soon. It was just another tough moment in a wild decade for the institution founded in Scotland back in 1768.

Encyclopedia Britannica, like *Webster's Dictionary* and *Roget's Thesaurus*, is a pillar of the English-speaking world, but it had a rocky road because of the PC and the Web. Microsoft's *Encarta* took the market by storm, offering an OK product at a much cheaper price, all condensed on a CD-ROM to be called up as needed on one's computer. *Britannica* ditched its famous door-to-door salesmen, started minting CD-ROMs, and began offering online subscriptions; yet the market leader remained stuck in second place. The only remaining step was to give the product away. Digitized encyclopedias succeed for the same reason the Bible software industry and Internet search engines keep growing. People like having indexed collections available so a tidbit can be found when needed. Today's high-capacity data storage offers all the benefits of being a pack rat without the clutter. It also makes literacy cheap.

Perhaps more importantly in the long run, scholarly journals are increasingly going online. Such publications are absolutely essential in the academic, scientific, and medical worlds, printing the latest research so that other scholars in the field can draw on their colleagues' discoveries. But by the nature of specialization, not that many people subscribe to them and there are not enough experts to turn a profit. Libraries take them, but because of the lack of economy of scale they are very expensive, and they take up lots and lots of shelf space. Now academic journals are going online. The cost of paper and distribution is nothing. They take up no space at all. And yet every library, every expert, every researcher can have instant access to the information.

Not only that, online journals are actually better than the hard copies because they can be completely up-to-date. Traditionally since time immemorial, scholarly journals have always been published as quarterlies, coming out, quaintly, one per season (Winter, Spring, Summer, and Fall). But in fast-moving fields such as science and medicine, a journal that comes out only every three months can be obsolete before it goes in the mail. But with online journals—and the increasing custom by which scholars post their work themselves on their own sites—important articles can be accessed instantly. Research can now be completely up-to-date.

When avant-garde French philosophers and literary professors started the ongoing debate about postmodernity, they never expected the massive explosion that came from Tim Berners-Lee's invention of hypertext. Now every idea, movement, class, race, and ethnicity can have its voice after all. Sure, some greedy capitalist can exploit the proletariat, but the workers can always get anonymous web pages to expose their plight. At least in free-speech-oriented countries—and with the new media it is increasingly difficult to prevent free speech, even when tyrannical governments want to—there will always be an outlet for people to talk—about their cats, their favorite bands, or the writings of

Groen Van Prinsterer. The Web allows people to hunt down their hobbies and secret passions, all by themselves, sitting behind a screen.

A CALL FOR CHRISTIANS

To manage the torrent of information, a person needs criteria, a method of discernment, a worldview. These are some of the few things that the Internet in itself cannot deliver.

This is where Christianity comes in. Since everything is possible, there's nothing stopping Christians from breaking new ground. The cost of expression will meet anyone's budget. Every church has an ongoing collection of content called sermons. There are hundreds of important Christian books sitting neglected in libraries or microfilm drawers. Why not bring them out for a new generation? There are Christian critiques of social evils and philosophical falsehoods, critiques that now cannot be silenced by agnostic gatekeepers in academia or the media.

And again, Christians can keep their own gates. Christian communities can come together online. As a means of mass communication, the Web offers a way of communicating, among other things, the Gospel of Christ. Though the Web is no substitute for a real church and real, face-to-face Christian fellowship, and though it poses problems and temptations of its own, it is a tool that Christians, individually and collectively, can make good use of, making Christianity once again a player in the marketplace of ideas.

The Tangled Web We Weave

The Good and the Bad
of the Internet

CHAPTER FIVE

The Internet as a Conserving Activity

New media reverberates throughout the culture. As always, the changes from a media revolution have two sides from a Christian point of view, one positive and one negative. While the printing press disseminated God's Word on an unparalleled scale, it also made possible the interior speculations that would give us the anti-Christian Enlightenment. While the telegraph obliterated distance and tied isolated communities in with the rest of the wide world, it also weakened the identity and the self-sufficiency of individual localities. While television gives us unprecedented immediate access to news, entertainment, drama, and sports, it has also spawned a decadent pop culture that is making us shallow and intellectually lazy.

In the mainline cultural establishment today—in the press, the universities, the art circles, and among other culture makers—Christianity hardly exists except as a reflection of bad old times or as a sentimental memento. The Enlightenment and the modernists, confident with their age of reason and scientific materialism, banished Christianity from the public square. Partly in response, many American evangelicals retreated into a tightly guarded subculture as a world of mass media developed around them. Soon they were seen as exotic and scary to the dominant media culture, which began painting them with the broad and demonizing "Religious Right" brush. Many bookstores today stock only a hazy amount of Christian fare, and often only the Classical section of a record store reflects the work of believers.

But on the Net the old prejudices can be washed away. As with other mass media, it is another double-sided blessing. Certainly the temptations and distortions opened up by this new media are cause for concern, and we will discuss them in the next chapter. But there is much in the new media that social conservatives should applaud. In fact, the Internet has the potential of undermining much of the modernist secularism and the liberal politics that have dominated most of the twentieth century.

For example, the academic establishment that has so effectively kept Christianity out of the marketplace of ideas can no longer enforce its monopoly over the means of intellectual production. They still control the classrooms, but they no longer control serious discourse. Even their monopoly in the classrooms is being challenged, at least on one level, by the plethora of homeschoolers who, with the help of online resources and Internet tutorials, are finding they can outperform the public schools at their own game. The Internet breaks down the role of cultural gatekeepers—the program directors, editors, publicists, and moguls who help determine popular fashion. While those people will always be around, they can't stop a sharp person with a Christian worldview from getting his or her message out. And Christians can even move into abandoned gates, offering a perspective that can impose order on the chaotic matter of the Internet universe.

The Internet is also undermining the very possibility of a mass culture, making possible the catering to specific tastes rather than to the lowest possible denominator of the TV-bred pop culture. This means that Christians will no longer be at the mercy of Hollywood, with its debased tastes and the undermining of their values. Rather, Christians will be in a position to create counter-progamming of their own.

Free-market capitalism, opposed by chic socialists and government controllers for most of the twentieth century, is not only dominant in the information age, but is reaching a form more pure and more immediate than Adam Smith could have dreamed. Totalitarianism of every kind is more difficult, given the Internet. Politics is changed as once-ignored voices—such as those of Christians—can now be heard. Highly-centralized governments are unthinkable now, as the Internet makes everything decentralized. The new technology enshrines what has always been a political conservative's ideal—individual liberty.

The Internet is essentially a democratic medium. Though it is prone to the same dangers as pure democracy—from demagoguery to releasing the passions of the multitude—it also embodies many of the classic American virtues—individualism, liberty, dreams of success through personal enterprise.

And not only does the Internet promote liberty, it also promotes what is often seen as its opposite but is actually another conservative goal—community. Individuals lost in the fragmentation of the twentieth century are now able to join together into relationships—"networks"—once again. These relationships are not limited to one locale; rather, people now can connect with like-minded people from around the world. As we will see, the Internet can strengthen even families, as the decentralized workplace enables fathers and mothers to spend time at home with their children, who in turn can be homeschooled with the help of the new technology.

If the good side of the Internet is the absence of gatekeepers, the building up of liberty, and the cultivation of community, the bad side of the Internet also has to do with the absence of gate-keepers, the rise of liberty, and its take on community. The lack of gatekeepers can mean that information is voluminous but meaningless, with no distinction between truth and falsehood, between what is valuable and what is a waste of time. The free-dom opened up by the Internet degenerates into license and moral corruption. Community degenerates into tribalism, exploitation, and escapism.

The key to a Christian appropriation of the Internet is to apply what Christianity has always taught about liberty, com-munity, and gatekeeping. Liberty finds its fulfillment through the cultivation of Christian freedom. To develop the Internet's potential for community-making without falling into its poten-tial for abuse requires the cultivation of Christian love. To take advantage of the lack of gatekeepers while developing a frame-work to filter out what is worthless requires the cultivation of Christian discernment.

Christians can build one another up with Christian art, cul-ture, theology, and other things one won't find on cable TV or at Waldenbooks. The dark side of the Internet and how Christians need to respond to a whole array of new temptations will be explored later. To focus only on the bad things—or even to avoid the Net entirely because of them—is a bad idea, an eva-sion of the challenge put before us, a rejection of the new oppor-tunity put in our laps to address the surrounding world with the truth of God's Word. We must recognize the sense in which this new technology is a blessing from God.

THE DEMISE OF THE GATEKEEPERS

The Constitution of the United States of America guarantees the freedom of the press. Book publishers, newspaper editors, and academic journals may print whatever they want to say without fear of government censorship. This liberty involves the freedom to be selective. Those who own the presses may choose what to print. Publishers do not have to put forth every idea that comes along. They make judgments about what is worth printing, according to their own philosophical assumptions and economic self-interest. This is what it means to have freedom of the press.

But what if you do not own a printing press? You may have a great idea, but it may never be heard unless someone else publishes it. That means jumping through hoops. If the person who owns the press is not pleased, your work won't find an audience. There are any number of reasons why the publisher might turn it down, keeping it from entering the marketplace of ideas opened up by the media revolution launched by the printing press. It might not sell. It might not be written well enough to meet the editors' high standards. It might not accord with the editors' beliefs. Maybe you can eventually find a publisher who agrees with you, or maybe you can go to the expense of printing the book yourself. But the owners of the printing press serve as gatekeepers, determining what gets published and what does not.

With the Internet, everyone, in effect, owns a printing press. Most accounts give away a few megabytes of disk space, enough for several standard-sized books. Beyond that, other companies give away Web space in exchange for tacking on ads. And even if a person can't afford a computer, schools and libraries often provide access to their terminals for free.

That means everyone has immediate, direct access to a mass

audience. This does not mean that the mass audience will flock to your web site to read your ideas. It does mean that individuals have a forum for their writings that does not depend on major investments in paper and ink.

The Internet does not mean that books are obsolete. It does mean that if you do end up self-publishing your book, you can place it on Amazon.com, where it can take its place next to the products of major New York publishing companies, giving your little book the same access to a major distribution pipeline. Amazon.com won't give you the promotion that the New York corporations get, but at least you have a running start. If all else fails, you can give your ideas away for free on your own web site.

Individuals with something to say can now go directly to an audience, without the intermediaries of publishers, editors, corporate investors, or peer reviewers. For the writer, there is still the challenge of building an audience, and for the readers there is the challenge of information overload. Nevertheless, the Internet is empowering for individuals with something to say.

This democratization of the freedom of the press is especially important for voices and ideas that have been marginalized. Like the snooty doorkeepers at fashionable clubs who hold back the crowds behind velvet ropes and choose who looks good enough to be allowed to go in, our cultural elite have kept out scruffy and uncool perspectives from getting into the cultural party. For the last century, Christians have been left behind the velvet rope.

The way academic journals work is that research is submitted; then, after initial screening by the editor, it is put before a panel of "peer reviewers." This consists of other experts in the field, who determine if the submitted work is legitimate and if it deserves publication. On the one hand, this is an excellent system, ensuring that what a medical journal, for example, prints is consistent with good medicine and is generally reliable for other physicians to use. On the other hand, the system of peer review sets up something of a closed system, making it difficult for a way of thinking that is radically different from that of the peer reviewers to break in.

Another limiting factor with academic journals is, again, that they usually only publish four times a year. Paper and print are expensive, and space is limited. Naturally the editors do have to be highly selective about what they include. Many good papers, with high marks from the peer reviewers, never make it in, just because something that seems more important has a higher claim on the space. Thus print technology artificially, as well as purposefully, limits the ideas and information that go into larger circulation.

In the academic world, "publish or perish" means that professors and scholars must be always contributing new research and new ideas, which must gain the recognition and professional circulation ensured by publication. But this means going through a gauntlet of people who could keep that from happening. The system works best in medicine and the hard sciences, where the commitment to objective truth is high. In the social sciences and humanities, where worldview issues are directly at stake, the biases of modernism (leaving out the very possibility of supernatural truth) and postmodernism (claiming that truth is relative) have been more obvious.

Not just Christian scholars but social and political conservatives in general have felt their ideas to be excluded by the academic establishment. Marxist interpretations of art, literature, and culture are still respected—despite the implosion of Soviet communism—but a bit of scholarship that casts doubt on the claims of feminists or homosexuals or Darwinists could hardly get printed today in a mainline academic journal. To be sure, "unapproved" perspectives have given birth to journals of their own, but these seldom have the clout or influence of the major professional journals.

The Internet, though, is changing the whole structure of academic research. The expensive hard-copy quarterlies are being displaced by "electronic journals." The results of experiments, new evidence, and new interpretations can now be posted electronically, making them available to others in the field who have only to download the new research into their computers. The most prestigious of the e-journals are still peer-reviewed, ensuring a measure of reliability and quality control; but they can make available many more articles and much more research than the paper journals could ever manage.

Moreover, as has been said, e-journals can be up-to-date. An article submitted to a journal could take months to get accepted, more months to be peer-reviewed, only to have to wait its turn until there is room for it in either the Spring, Summer, Fall, or Winter issue. Since it may take a year or more for an article to get in print, it is often outdated by the time it appears. Now cancer researchers, for example, can have the latest information at their fingertips, immediately, when they need it. There are now no artificial limitations to the acquisition of knowledge.

Another change is that the scholarly enterprise is now taking place apart from the fixed products of journal publication. Now information and discussion are shared instantaneously as scholars communicate with each other via E-mail and discussion lists. This represents a kind of collaboration that was formerly only possible among colleagues working together in a lab or on a campus. Now scholars can collaborate on a global scale. Everyone working in a particular area can, potentially, be colleagues and coworkers with each other.

In the meantime data, information, and papers—published

elsewhere or not—can just be posted on a web site, passed around electronically and discussed from person to person, and transmitted instantly, available to the whole scholarly community.

This bodes well for the advancement of knowledge as a whole. It is also something Christian scholars can take advantage of. E-journals and discussion lists can be forums for the development of scholarship that emanates from a biblical worldview (in the most wide-ranging sense of that term, which embraces even the so-called secular fields). In addition, the withering away of academic gatekeepers, made possible by the new technology, allows Christian and other lesser-heard perspectives back into the mainstream.

It has been said that the relative anonymity of the Internet, in which people are known mainly by their screen names, is a great intellectual and social leveler. One's degrees or academic affiliation mean little on an E-mail discussion list. What matters is being able to make one's case. The end of the gatekeepers opens up possibilities for Christian thinkers to become players again. But it is still necessary to go through the gates.

THE END OF THE MASS CULTURE

Without the usual gatekeepers, not only is the intellectual scene more dynamic, with greater chances for participation, but the whole culture—from politics to the arts—is opened up in a similar way. In fact, at hand, eventually, may be what conservatives have long yearned for—the end of the pop culture.

Time was, "the media" was pretty much monolithic. There were three television networks, which differed little from each other. A few major newspapers, aided by a few "wire services" from which nearly every paper got their stories, shaped the whole nation's understanding of current events.

Conservatives railed against "the liberal media," with its Democratic bias, its championing of "progressive" causes, and its indifference to "traditional" moral values. Such bias is still evident in the mainstream press (note the figure of speech, calling attention to the way journalists have been tied to a printing press). But now, having a printing press or its broadcasting equivalent is no longer the issue.

Now news passes directly from E-mail account to E-mail account. It is much harder to keep anything quiet. The conservative voice—and information that proves conservatives' points—cannot be shut up.

President Kennedy's sexual adventures were discreetly passed over by the sympathetic journalists who covered the White House. President Clinton might have enjoyed similar treatment were it not for the Internet. The story of the President's affair with Monica Lewinsky and the cover-ups that led to his impeachment came out largely due to the efforts of Matt Drudge, a maverick pro-life conservative whose online reports—though scorned as gossip by many print journalists—were to the Clinton scandals what the *Washington Post* was to Watergate.

Today, due to the alternative media (which would also include talk radio), it is more difficult than ever for politicians and their allies to manage information and to manipulate the public.

Totalitarianism is more difficult now. The notion of a "total" government requires rigorous control of information, a vast propaganda machine to keep its citizens in line. The Soviet Union was busy jamming radio signals from outside and outlawed the private possession of a copy machine. But if the citizens have computers, they not only have access to information from the outside, they can share it—along with their own complaints of government outrages and their calls for freedom—with their fellow citizens. The role of the Internet in resisting tyrants has been evident since the breakup of the Soviet Union, including also the fall of various Third World dictators. Today the last bastion of totalitarian communism, China, is desperately—but futilely—trying to figure out how to control what comes into their country via the Internet.

The Internet promotes political liberty, allowing ordinary citizens to speak their minds and to organize, forming networks and taking actions that operate outside the easily controlled bounds of political parties and media advertising. The political implications of the Internet are well in accord with the virtues of a democratic republic—if, that is, citizens will tear themselves away from their computer screens sometimes to be aware of the real world all around them.

THE NEW PERSONAL MEDIA

The engine that has driven the pop culture—the commercialized, lowest-common-denominator-appeal-to-the dumbest entertainment culture—has been television. TV has been the nemesis of cultural conservatives in the way it has driven out reflection in favor of sensate images, hedonism, and anti-intellectual manipulation. The criterion for the success of a television program is neither aesthetic excellence nor moral impact, but ratings. Whatever can round up the largest audiences will thrive—and an easy way to do so is through the cheap and easy titillation of sex, violence, and mockery. This necessarily means undercutting moral principles and the kinds of attitudes and ways of thinking that families and societies have always needed to cultivate. Because the TV industry was relatively monolithic—controlled by a handful of people in a few corporations—there were not many options.

But now the newer technology is changing things. TV watching has dropped precipitously, especially in families that are online. Instead of passively absorbing video images, people are reading, writing, and seeing what they are tracking down for themselves. Though the entertainment mentality fostered by TV remains, Internet entertainment tends to be interactive rather than passive and one-way, often requiring the use of the individual intellect.

But even television itself is changing, thanks to the way the world is now wired. Now instead of having to watch only ABC, CBS, or NBC, cable and satellite subscribers have access to fifty or 100 or even more channels.

True, to fill so much airspace many of these cable networks rely on reruns of programs that were originally produced by the majors. But syndication has opened the door for independently produced programming. This exploding new demand for programming is a golden opportunity for Christians to find a place for themselves and for their beliefs on the newly opened bandwidths. And the technology is making it less and less expensive to do so.

But even more to the point, the multiplicity of viewing options now becoming possible will allow audiences to be completely selective in what they and their families view. "Broadcasting" is giving way to "narrowcasting." Instead of trying to reach a mass audience, the goal is to reach a specific audience. This is also the goal of advertisers, who are realizing that they need not spend vast sums to advertise on national television, in which they are paying to reach people who will never buy their product. Why advertise a Mercedes on *The Jerry Springer Show*? Much more efficient is to target their advertising spending so that it finds people who are actually potential customers. Those who might buy a Mercedes might be watching an opera on The Learning Channel, a kind of programming that once had to be carried only on PBS but now can attract the right kind of advertisers.

Not only is narrowcasting the new norm (a technological development that would have been impossible without the computer and today's wired information technology), but the fusion of TV with the Internet will give the viewer sovereign control over what comes over the wires into the living room. The viewer will be able to choose, from a nearly limitless menu, the programs he wants to see. And he can call them up anytime he wants.

If he wants to see *Gilligan's Island* reruns all day or construct an all *McGyver* channel, that will be his prerogative. If he is bothered by vulgar talk shows, comedies with sexual innuendoes, or programs that insult his faith and provide bad role models for his children, they need never come into his home. He can instead watch programs he believes in and that support his values. This assumes, of course, that there will be people to develop programming for this particular niche. And it assumes that Christian viewers will in fact watch the positive programming they clamor for, instead of indulging in their secret vice of enjoying the same decadent entertainment their non-Christian neighbors do.

Not that on-demand TV will solve our cultural problems. This total freedom of viewing will mean that voyeurs can use their online TVs for a constant fix of pornography in all its perverse varieties. And it may be that the vulgar masses will continue to pull the biggest market for sleazy talk shows. This medium will undoubtedly contribute to the fragmentation of our culture, into smaller and smaller interest groups that have less and less in common, and fewer and fewer of the social ties that every nation needs. And yet solid citizens must live with the pornography lurkers and others who abase their moral sensibilities online. But Christians can worry less about television corrupting their children if they use the technology well. Thoughtful people will have access to thoughtful programming. Those who love fine drama, with sophisticated themes and artistic production, should be able to find it. What will happen is that, both for better and for worse, our tastes and values and beliefs will be reflected in our own personal media.

THE FREE ECONOMY

What the Internet does, essentially, is decentralize. What was once in the hands of gatekeepers, big government, or monolithic corporations is now put in the hands of smaller communities and individuals, who nevertheless have a global reach. Decentralization has long been a goal of political and social conservatives, for whom a powerful, distant center of power has always been seen as a threat to individual and social liberties. Part of this conservative agenda has involved working for a decentralized economy—freed from state control and artificial manipulations—in which the laws of supply and demand, competition, and personal enterprise can function freely for the greater prosperity of everyone. This is exactly what the Internet, as it becomes more and more part of our economic infrastructure, allows to happen.

"Today's economy," says Alan Murray of the *Wall Street Journal*, "may be closer than ever to the theoretical models of capitalism that have existed in the minds of economists dating back to Adam Smith."[1] These models have assumed that human beings act in their rational self-interest, that economic forces are allowed to operate freely, and that markets are self-regulating. Though the economic laws worked out through these models have been vindicated time and time again, they do not always find application in the real world. Human beings are not always rational. Governments insist on regulating and trying to control the economy. Businesses and consumers do not always have the information they need to respond to market forces.

Human beings are still not always rational, as Christians well know; but the Internet empowers them, in new ways, to act in their own economic interests. The collapse of communism has been accompanied by the collapse of welfare state socialism and the triumph of global capitalism; the deregulated economies, many driven by the uncontrollable Internet, have soared. And the technologies of the "information age" make economic information available instantaneously, allowing for "frictionless commerce,"[2] in which the free market operates in a way that comes close to theoretical purity.

"Economists have long argued that 'imperfect information' is a major reason for economic malfunction," says Murray. "In the old economy, for instance, factories would crunch out products for months after demand had fallen off because they didn't know about the change. The classic result: bulging inventories, leading to an inventory correction and perhaps even recession. In the new economy, producers and consumers are wired, and everyone sees a drop in demand as it happens."[3] He gives the example of a lumber mill that monitors the latest prices for various cuts of boards. If the price goes up for two-by-fours, that means there is a shortage of them, so that's how they cut the logs. When the price goes down, that means the market is glutted with two-by-fours, whereupon the mill shifts its operation to make exactly what the market needs.

Theoretically, consumers would buy products that represent the best price and the highest quality. Companies would compete with each other to meet this consumer demand, adjusting prices for what the market would bear. Greater demand would bid up the price, while lesser demand could be stimulated by price cuts or by improvements in quality. In real life, though, a consumer going to a store has little knowledge of what competing stores might offer, unless the shopper has the time to drive all over town. Most prices are fixed by the price tag. A consumer can negotiate the price for big-ticket items like automobiles and real estate, but how many know what might be a reasonable offer? Most remain at the mercy of the car dealers, for example, who alone know what the car cost them and can adjust their profit margins according to the gullibility of the customer.

But with the Internet, consumers have access to economic information, so that different companies selling a product actually do have to compete with each other, and the dynamics of supply, demand, and pricing can work as Adam Smith had in mind. Now a customer can check the Web to compare prices and offerings from a wide range of companies. The customer is no longer bound by geography, being able to buy not just from local businesses but from businesses across the country or around the world, as well as from companies that are located only in cyberspace.

To buy a car today, a customer can draw on a host of web sites that will give the dealer's invoice cost and that will allow dealers to compete for his business. Some sites allow the customer to enter in the make, model, and features of the car that he would like to buy (the various specifications for which are also easily found on the Web). He types in his zip code, whereupon car companies (whether in his area or based only on the Web) can make their offers. The customer can compare prices, let the rival dealers compete with each other, or simply go to his local dealer, name the price he got on the Internet, and ask the dealer to match it.

What works for buying cars also works for buying books, medicine, electronic equipment, and even groceries. "No longer can the corner druggist or the local mall's bookshop demand huge markups for their wares," observes economics reporter Jacob Schlesinger. "Shoppers have two powerful new weapons—information about what competitors around the country are charging for the same goods, and easy access to those goods online if the nearby merchant won't deal."[4] He quotes economist Ethan Harris, who points out that "the Internet eliminates local monopoly power."[5]

Perhaps the purest example of pricing according to supply and demand is the phenomenon of Internet auctions. On a number of sites, products are put up for sale. Those interested in buying them put in a bid. If the demand is high—if many buyers are competing against each other and so keep raising their bids—the price naturally goes up. Buyers end up paying exactly what the product is worth as determined by market forces.

On a larger scale, helping the companies themselves make more money while offering competitive prices, fewer middlemen are needed, and less bricks-and-mortar investment. An immaterial web site can do the business of innumerable shops, employees, and strip malls. Marvin Zonis, a business professor at the University of Chicago, says that the Net is driving down "transaction costs"—the multiple layers of administrative and retail overhead that adds so much to the price of doing business.[6] Physical goods still need to be delivered, which is now feasible on a global scale thanks to computer-assisted mail and express and delivery services; but otherwise, he points out, distance becomes obsolete.

All of this amounts to huge increases in economic efficiency and in economic productivity. The instant market information, the "frictionless" transactions, the competitive dynamics that end up increasing quality while reducing price—all of this allows the unfettered marketplace to perform its wonders, just as Adam Smith said it would.

"The emerging internet economy," according to economists Andrew Whinston and Anitesh Barua, "is similar to the Industrial Revolution that began in the 18th century in potential scope, size and overall economic impact."[7] To be sure, we are in a very early stage of this alleged revolution. People are just now getting used to buying things by clicking onto an icon. The role of credit and the credit card in this new economy isn't always factored in or its implications clearly understood—the usurious interest rates charged on every transaction might prove an economic drag. As of this writing, only 1 percent of retail sales are happening online.[8] And yet, online commerce has already surpassed the annual revenue of airlines and the telecommunications industry. The rate of growth of the Internet economy is twenty times that of brick-and-mortar businesses. Economists look for it to quadruple in three years.

Christians should always be skeptical of utopian claims. The same factors that messed up industrial capitalism—government regulation, monopolies, rigged markets, labor exploitation, and sheer greedy corruption—may well mess up the Internet economy. But in the meantime no one can deny that it has increased productivity and efficiency and that its economic dynamism should warm a conservative's heart.

PRESERVING THE CULTURAL INFRASTRUCTURE

But the most positive implication, from a social conservative's point of view, of the new economy is that its benefits do not extend only to the big players, the Silicon Valley corporations and the venture capital investors. It decentralizes its benefits to the point that ordinary individuals—with their small businesses and private enterprises—have the same ability to take advantage of its economic potential for themselves. The effect is to build up social institutions—from small towns to the family itself—that have long been under siege.

Farmers, for example, are a much-beleaguered group, regularly pounded by economic forces beyond their control, despite their crucial importance in feeding the rest of us and despite the cultural value of the family farm. Most industries and most workers profit by increased productivity, but farmers who increase their yields end up creating a glutted market, driving prices down, so that they actually can lose money when they produce more. Adam Smith's law of supply and demand has tended to work against farmers, who have little control over such things and thus often find themselves strangled by "the invisible hand." (This is why farmers, despite their sturdy family values, tend to vote for liberal, control-the-economy politicians.)

Today, though, farmers are taking advantage of the Internet. They are no longer at the mercy of the grain buyer, having to accept the going rate for their harvest, however glutted the market may be that day. Rather, the Internet lets them monitor the market; they store their grain, and then when prices are up, they sell. Farmers are also buying seed, insecticide, fertilizer, and other supplies online. By eliminating the various levels of wholesalers and retailers and by scouring the virtual suppliers for the best prices, they can cut their costs and squeeze out a higher profit margin that can keep them in business.[9]

The Internet is also contributing to the conservation of old-time American culture by revitalizing the small town. Heavy industries and centralized corporations needed to be grouped together in big cities. Being huddled together in the same urban locale made it easier to communicate with their various operations. Big businesses also tended to locate close to their customer base. The city became the place where there were more jobs, and the population growth meant more shops and services and even more economic activity, centered in the city. This growth came at the expense of small towns, which lost population and economic vitality, while urban areas kept getting bigger and, in some ways, more unlivable.

The invention of the interstate highway and the rise of the automobile culture changed the urban landscape. People could live in the more agrarian suburbs and drive into the city to work. Before long, businesses and factories themselves moved out to the suburbs.

Now small-town business owners are finding that they can compete with the big boys by means of the Web. Used book dealers, quirky music stores, candy shops, and other tiny niche dealers are finding that the Web allows them to tap into a vast market far beyond their city limits. According to Kennedy Smith, head of the National Main Street Center at the National Trust for Historic Preservation, "Main Street businesses are now doing 20% or 40% of their sales from their Web sites." "Businesses don't need their customer base within a 50-mile radius," he says. "Overnight delivery and the Internet have set them free."[10] Said the owner of a music store who is finding that he can compete against the big chains, "It's like being a big-box store without being a big box."[11]

The issue is not just the virtue of small towns. In a wired-together world, individuals can live wherever they want to. *World Magazine*, for example—with which both of the authors of this book are associated—offers a Christian-informed perspective to the news that is a stark alternative to the mainline press. *World*'s offices are in Asheville, North Carolina, but the chief editor lives in Austin, Texas; the Managing Editor lives in St. Louis; and other editors and writers are scattered across the country—Seattle, Los Angeles, Washington, and little towns from Wisconsin to Texas. The far-flung writers can thus cover and are closer to a wide range of on-the-spot stories. Each week stories are written from across the country, then submitted to the editors via the Internet. After being edited and set into virtual pages—with the use of publishing software—by the various editors, each in a different city, the page files are forwarded, again by the Internet, for more electronic assembly. Finally the electronic file for the whole issue is sent to the printing company—again, by Internet—where the magazine is manufactured and mailed to its 100,000 subscribers. Without the Internet, *World* would not be possible.

The economic and social decentralization made possible by the Internet can be profoundly liberating for enterprising individuals, who now have the technological and institutional firepower that was once available only to huge corporations.

Twenty-nine-year-old movie buff Greg Dean Schmitz worked as a Reference Librarian at the Oshkosh Public Library in rural Wisconsin. He designed a web site (www.upcomingmovies.com) in which he posted his thoughts about new and upcoming movies. He kept it simple, avoiding all of the graphics that take so long to download, and made a point of reviewing movies without spoiling the plots by revealing too much information about what happens. He began specializing in garnering information about upcoming movies, giving previews, release dates, and industry buzz, which he uncovered by means, of course, of the Internet. Today his site attracts one and a half million hits per month. With this kind of audience, it didn't take much advertising to enable him to quit his job as a librarian, freeing him to devote full time to his web site.[12]

Columnist Thomas Friedman tells about book lover Lyle Bowlin of Cedar Falls, Iowa, who started competing with

Amazon.com from a spare bedroom. He found that he could get the same discounts from wholesalers by ordering just five copies of a particular book. He started a web site (www.positively-you.com). He paid an Internet service provider $30 a month to host his web site. Thirty more dollars to another Internet business, Americart, allowed people to charge purchases on their credit cards via a secure line. His bank charged $50 a month to handle the credit card transactions. He also spends $40 for a monthly newsletter. Total overhead: $150 per month.

"I have no employees," he said. "My daughter does the accounting, I maintain the Web site and my wife does the shipping. Altogether, I only need to generate $150 a month in profits to cover all my expenses, and the rest is cream."

He even found that he could undercut Amazon.com's prices. Both of them could get a 44 percent discount off books from the wholesaler. Amazon can offer 30 percent off. Mr. Bowlin, who has even less overhead than Amazon, offered a 35 percent discount. He also saved shipping costs by using the U.S. Postal Service and their three-day delivery. His web site promised "Millions of Books at Great Prices"—and in fact, he could get access to just about any of the myriad of books that have been published. But he did not need a warehouse to store them all in, only his bedroom. And while Amazon.com is a $23.6 billion company that loses $375 million a year, Mr. Bowlin, who only had to make $150 to start making profits, operated in the black and did quite nicely.[13]

Ironically, his business was doomed by its success. As more and more people wanted to buy from his site—encouraged by Friedman's article—he grew his enterprise to meet the demand. Before long, he was big enough to have the problems of scale faced by Amazon. Mr. Bowlin has since shut down the business, gone back to teaching, and taken his spare bedroom back. But his experience shows what is possible.

Christian author Nancy Pearcey has pointed out how the new information technology can help parents spend more time with their children, reversing a centuries-old trend.[14] Before industrialism, she points out, most families worked in their homes. Fathers, mothers, and children all worked together on the farm and in the household. As they pursued the economic necessities of life—not only as farmers but as craftsmen and shopkeepers who also worked out of their homes—they spent lots of time together, pulling together as a family in a common effort. With the Industrial Revolution, however, work became divorced from the home. Men—and sometimes women and even children—would leave home to work in the factories. Eventually a division of labor grew up, in which men would work outside the home, with women tending to the children, who themselves would leave home for school. With feminism in this century, women too insisted on the right to work outside the home. As a result, no one was left at home. The economic structures of industrialism, she argues, worked against the family, with fathers and eventually mothers spending less time with their children.

But now, thanks to the new information technology, it is possible once again to work at home. Both men and women are able to work at their computers, whether as independent web businesses or wired to a central office. The telecommuting made possible by the Internet and its economic and logistical decentralization is allowing more and more mothers to earn income while staying home with their children. It is also allowing fathers to earn income while staying home with their children and their wives. Not that all families have access to these kinds of opportunities, and certainly we are a long way from these social changes on a large scale. Still, the Internet has the potential of actually strengthening families.

Many Christian parents are pursuing homeschooling as an alternative to the moral, spiritual, and even academic bankruptcy of much contemporary education. They are often finding the Internet to be a great help, thanks to online tutorials and the host of educational materials their children can access and study at home.

It is a great paradox, of course, that this new technology is in effect making possible once again the family conditions of pre-industrial times. But the Internet, for all of its newness and its revolutionary changes—and for all of its problems, which we will discuss next—has a way of undoing at least some of the cultural damages wreaked by modernism. It is a tool that Christians can use in their project of rebuilding the culture.

CHAPTER SIX

The Dark Side of the Internet

🌀

At fourteen she finally joined the twenty-first century. Her father finally set up his AOL account so she could have a screen name of her own. Now she could surf the Web for her studies, E-mail her friends, and expand her horizons. She knew to be careful though. She would only go into "Christian" chat rooms. She found some chat rooms on AOL for fellow Christian teenagers, which allowed young people from all over the world to discuss their problems, pray for each other, and discuss theology far into the night.

But it wasn't long before she discovered that other individuals were skulking around in those chat rooms. It wasn't just Christians or teenagers who were interested in making contact with Christian teenaged girls. Satanists regularly showed up to mock, blaspheme, and flame the pious young people. So did sexual trawlers with their suave pick-up lines, such as "What are you wearing?" And so did out and out child molesters, angling to form trusting relationships with young girls.

She quit the chat rooms, but she kept getting mass E-mails from the predatory sorts who had access to the screen names and member profiles. She kept up her personal E-mail correspondence, which, as with many teenagers, soon included forwarded posts that were sent from friend to friend until they proliferated like a contagious illness. Soon professional pornographers got into the act, sending ads for nude photos, live sex video-cam web sites, and members-only porn sites with lots of free samples. She never responded to any of it, never sampled any of their wares. But now the first thing she does when she logs on to her E-mail account is to delete all of the pornographic spam.

The Internet may be a conserving activity in some ways, but it is also a realm in which perversion roams free, a morality-free zone in which inhibitions are short-circuited, human relationships can be twisted, and lies are indistinguishable from truth. We have argued that the benefits of the new technology include the way it increases our freedom, makes possible new forms of community, and eliminates the gatekeepers. The dangers of the new technology are shadows of its benefits: It increases freedom to the point of depraved moral license; it creates false communities that are actually isolating instead of communal; it eliminates gatekeepers that are needed.

The Internet, like any tool, seems to maximize what human beings can do. Since human beings are fallen, this includes acts of sin. It seems as if every technology opens up new possibilities for sinning. The transition from bronze to steel tools meant new efficiencies in killing; the printing press made possible pornographic novels; the automobile gave teenagers a portable, private room of their own for drinking-and-driving and back-seat sex; and on and on. Christians must always come to terms with the moral dimensions and the new moral challenges of new technologies. That technologies can be abused by no means implies that Christians cannot use them in a positive way. But they need to be wary. A realistic appropriation of any technology involves an assessment of both its capacity for good and its capacity for harm.

Christians need to confront the dark side of the Internet—not to be afraid of it, but to mitigate its problematic tendencies and to find ways of approaching it with discipline, discernment, and a sanctified imagination. In doing so, they will find that their biblical worldview provides a filtering mechanism that allows them to navigate through the informational deluge and that the Christian freedom given by the Gospel allows them to exploit the Internet without being caught in the net of sin.

AN INHIBITIONS-FREE ZONE

Morality, historically, is enforced by culture. Societies would be impossible if everyone is tearing each other apart; families, the basic unit of society, would be impossible if everyone is busy fornicating with everyone in sight. In theological terms, the first use of the Law is to restrain evil, so that sinful human beings can live in the company of each other in some measure of peace. Whatever sinful desires we might harbor deep inside due to our fallen nature, we tend to be ashamed to act upon them in public. If we do, the police are at hand to keep us in line, at least from the most socially harmful kinds of acting out. For the others, less criminal but no less damning, we are inhibited by shame and embarrassment or their more noble corollaries, self-respect and honor.

The fear of being recognized—"what if someone sees me?"—specifically, the fear of being identified, of having one's name and reputation exposed and sullied—has kept many sinners away from the old pornographic movie houses. Videos, though, can be enjoyed in the privacy of one's own home or hotel room, private spaces with little chance of recognition or embarrassment; and because of this, the pornography industry has been flourishing. Anonymity encourages the relaxing of inhibitions; what one might do in a far-off country where "nobody knows me" may be quite different from what one might do in one's own home town. This applies not only to sexual sins but to other vices. Anonymous letters tend to be far more vicious than those that are signed. The masked criminal tends to be the most brutal.

An individual's presence on the Internet consists only of a screen name, which need not have any connection with one's real name. The screen name—unlike an actual name—has no social context, representing no family, with no community ties or obligations. In cyberspace one can function apart from any fixed identity, surfing in total anonymity, where no one knows who you really are. Not having an identity, of course, can be very liberating. The relative anonymity—or at least the illusion of anonymity, since actually, as we shall see, the Internet is not a private place at all—encourages the shedding of inhibitions.

Communication via E-mail can be startlingly open, honest, and intimate, even with those who could be considered complete strangers; the inhibitions against self-disclosure are weakened apart from an actual social context. But so are the inhibitions against rudeness and hurting other people. Thus E-mail communication is also rife with flaming, unrestrained furious, profane invective, language that the person would probably never use addressing another person face to face.

Christians should not be surprised to find that in the absence of inhibitions, what emerges out of the murky depths of the human heart is the basest, most pathetic, and most sordid of vices—particularly sexual fantasies, perversions, and the thrill of transgression.

Porn on the Web has become a billion-dollar industry, making it one of the relatively few online enterprises that has been turning a profit from the beginning. Purveyors of pornography have become some of the biggest-spending advertisers on the Web. And they are certainly finding their audience. For all of the over-18 warnings and filtering programs, 25 percent of teenagers have visited X-rated sites.[1]

The Internet's true innovation in human sexuality, however, comes not so much from the commercial pornographers but from "virtual sex." Individuals cruise the chat rooms like lounge lizards in a singles bar, hitting on women ("What are you wearing?") or perhaps, unwittingly, on those pretending to be women. Upon finding a willing partner, they retire to a private chat room or an instant message box. They then type in what they are fantasizing doing to the other person, full of naughty words and upper-case moans, culminating in the release of self-gratification.

Some are hailing this as the ultimate form of "safe sex." In this age of AIDS, unwanted pregnancies, and sexual abuse, virtual sex offers the possibility of a sexual relationship with another person without having to worry about the body. Indeed, the old canards of attractiveness, of having to look good to impress someone of the opposite sex, disappear. The other person never sees you. No one has to worry about getting a sexually-transmitted disease, much less getting pregnant. The other person never so much as touches you. There is a sort of intimacy with another person—the flirtation, the seduction, the conquest—but there is no actual relationship. You don't even have to bother going out on dates.

True, the other person might not even have the gender you are fantasizing about. There is good reason to believe that men enjoy these fantasy games more than women do, and that a good number of the cyberlounge lizards are picking up other men. But again, that doesn't matter since the sex is all in one's head, a private self-pleasuring, so that the other person's body makes no difference at all. For some, this sexual preference represents the next step in human sexual liberation. In this age that is finally accepting homosexuality and transgendered sexual identities, they say, we can at last, through the aid of technology, transcend gender differences. Each person is free to take on whatever sexual identity he or she chooses, changing it at will, so that the whole range of sexual experience can be enjoyed.

What is wrong with this? No one—including one's virtual sex partner—gets hurt, it is said. There are no consequences. It is all just pretend, after all. It isn't really fornication or adultery. No one can get pregnant. It cannot lead to an abortion. Isn't virtual sex at most a virtual sin, not a real sin? How are we to answer this?

Well, for a start, Christ Himself says that sinfulness has to do precisely with what is happening in the mind. The sin is not just committing adultery, He says, but committing adultery in one's heart (Matthew 5:27-28).

More broadly, virtual sex represents not the next step in sexual liberation, but the next step in the wrenching of sex from God's design. God created sex for the engendering of children, in marriage, for the establishment of families. Note what has happened over the course of the sexual revolution: Contraceptive technology makes it possible to have sex without having children. Whether or not contraceptives are morally permissible, it is surely true that they have separated sex from both its biological purpose and its role in the family. So, if sex is just a pleasurable sensation without biological consequences, why not have sex outside of marriage? Why not enjoy this sensation in other non-fertile contexts, such as with someone of the same gender?

Sex is a near-miraculous function of the human body that

ends in the birth of new human beings. God could have created new generations of human beings from the dust, said Luther,[2] but He chose to bring new life into the world through husbands and wives becoming parents. Sex has to do with the bodies of a man and a woman, a loving and committed relationship between them, and the child that together they engender. What has happened is that sex has been divorced from having children, then from marriage. The Internet makes possible the further divorce of sex from any kind of human relationship and, finally, the divorce of sex from the body itself. All that is left is an isolated individual pretending to be someone else, alone, stimulating him- or herself in front of a computer screen.

This is surely sexual sin, but it is so wretched, so pathetic, that it almost inspires pity rather than indignation. How far such isolation, loneliness, and sterility is from God's design, in which sex is intended to promote life, relationships, and love. This may be seen as God's judgment against our abuse of His gift, a fatal "giving them what they want" that can be the worst punishment.

> *Therefore God gave them over in the sinful desires of their hearts to sexual impurity for the degrading of their bodies with one another. They exchanged the truth of God for a lie, and worshiped and served created things rather than the Creator—who is forever praised. Amen. Because of this, God gave them over to shameful lusts. Even their women exchanged natural relations for unnatural ones. In the same way the men also abandoned natural relations with women and were inflamed with lust for one another. Men committed indecent acts with other men, and received in themselves the due penalty for their perversion.*
>
> *—Romans 1:24-27*

Preferring lies to truth (think of the contrast between what is virtual and what is real) and serving things that are created rather than the Creator (think of enslavement to a machine) leads to God giving us over to "shameful lusts" and the trading of "natural" sexuality for "unnatural" relations. St. Paul, meet the twenty-first century.

It may seem ironic, but today's characteristic sexual sins involve an almost gnostic rejection of the body. A Christian view of sex, on the other hand, affirms the body in all its biological design, as God's handiwork.

THE POSTHUMAN

Certainly the dangers of the Internet are not merely of the virtual variety. Many are the cases in which adolescents have been lured into meetings in the real world with someone with whom they have had an online relationship, only to become victims of child molesters or other sexual criminals. Real-life marriages have been broken over virtual affairs.

And the evil actions made possible by this new technology are by no means limited to sexual vice. Internet term paper mills are making it easier to cheat. Internet scams—from phony investment schemes to credit card fraud—are making it easier to steal. Gambling has become a major Internet application, as it is now possible to evade local laws by logging onto an offshore server on a Caribbean island and bet on games until your credit card is maxed out. There is no limit to human ingenuity when it comes to finding new ways and new technology for sinning.

But it is this private, mental universe—the realm of self-consciously manufactured illusions, free of space and physicality and identity and presence—that constitutes the true dark side of the Internet. Christians with a strong sense of the creation, the Incarnation, redemption, and sanctification, grounded in the actual living community of a church, need not fear this dark side, though they would do well to note the temptations so they can avoid them. But the Internet, as an expression of late twentieth and early twenty-first century cultures, does indeed embody the worldviews of its age.

The Internet does promote community—enabling people to meet kindred spirits, develop friendships around common interests, and start relationships that can end in love and marriage. But the virtual community fostered by the Internet can also be artificial, an escape from genuine communities with their networks of responsibilities and social norms, into small, homogenous groups whose members feed each other's worst tendencies. What were once private idiosyncrasies or vices can now find support and reinforcement in groups of like-minded souls on the Web. Some of these can be wholly innocent—fans of TV shows, hobbyists, and book lovers (though the Web allows them to ride their hobby horses perhaps more than they are worth, taking time and mental energy away from more worthwhile pursuits). Others can be vicious—hate groups, cultists, kiddie porn aficionados (all of whom offer mutual support and consolation to their brethren).

Virtual communities can be entirely false. In his novel *Microserfs*, about the wage slaves of Silicon Valley, Douglas Coupland tells the tale of a young man who falls in love on the Internet. After a long time of communicating online, the couple decide to meet. As the days and hours pass until the appointed time, the young man is in torment, hoping and praying that the person he has come to love will turn out to be a woman.

The Internet is a realm of role-playing and identity shifting. You think you know the person you have become friends with, but you just can't be sure. Role-playing games are, in fact, a specialty of the Net. In the various fantasy "multi-user dungeons," with real-seeming visuals and computer graphics, it is possible to interact with other players—and to fight them and kill them. One may play the part of a warrior, a wizard, a thief, or even a rapist, lurking in the 3-D alleyways, ready to pounce upon a victim.

But even when not playing games, the tendency is to adopt different persona when doing different things on the Web. Internet providers allow a single account to have many screen names, and each one often stands for a different personality. One may be for public business. Another may be reserved for signing onto porn sites. A man might choose to use a female screen name to achieve greater popularity in the chat rooms.

Some Internet utopians are hailing this freedom to assume different identities. It ties into the ideal of the "Protean self" of postmodern psychology, which denies that anyone should have one consistent identity, valuing instead limitless flexibility and constant self-reinvention.[3] Who we are depends on the group we are in, say the postmodernists, and since the Internet lets us be part of any number of groups, we can have different selves for them all. This, they say, is ultimate freedom—freedom not only from moral constraints, but freedom from one's own identity. Not to mention freedom from one's body.

Some avant-garde thinkers, looking ahead to what will come after postmodernism, are lauding what they are calling "the posthuman."[4] This is the point at which we are finally freed from biological constraints, including the mind's bondage to the body. The posthuman will include the merger of human life with the machine. Reproductive technology and genetic engineering will mean that human beings will no longer have to bear children. When babies are routinely conceived in petri dishes and brought to term in artificial wombs, women will achieve their final liberation. The biological and cultural distinctions between men and women—and the consequent oppression of women by men—will be no more. Not only homosexuality but bisexuality and cross-gendered sexual experiences will become the norm once virtual sex is perfected, not just in chat rooms but as multidimensional sensory illusions. With the help of the Internet, individuals will become known only through their minds.

These minds, say the cyber-utopians, can merge with other minds in new modes of community, unfettered by individual differences and physical limitations. Some consider the human mind nothing more than electrical information and the brain nothing more than a great "meat computer" no different in kind from the man-made kind built out of silicon and plastic. It should thus be possible for all individual human minds to merge together into a collective consciousness, they say, as individual cells join together to form a single sentient organism, just as individual computer chips function together as one machine. Then there is the project dreamed up by Timothy Leary on his deathbed—downloading one's mind and consciousness onto the Internet. If this could be done, the body could go ahead and die, and one could achieve everlasting life.

Being freed from the body and from the physical creation itself, existing as pure, unfettered mind, has a spiritual sound. But this is not Christian spirituality. Rather, it is a high-tech version of the ancient heresy of gnosticism. According to this eastern-influenced theology, which was battled by the early church, the physical realm is at best illusory and at worst evil. In the first of their blasphemies, they asserted that the Creator, the God of the Old Testament, is an evil deity because He created the physical universe. They also rejected the Incarnation, denying that "Jesus Christ has come in the flesh" (1 John 4:2); the Gnostics were the false prophets warned against in John's epistle. Jesus did not come in the flesh, they taught, nor was He crucified or raised bodily from the grave; rather, they said, Jesus was a spirit-being, a deity who would not be contaminated by being physical, who only *seemed* to die on the cross and whose resurrection was a purely spiritual, not physical, event. Salvation consisted of escape from this world through a direct, inner knowledge of God.

Gnostics do not need a mediator between themselves and the divine and so have no need of Christ, the Atonement, the Church, the sacraments, or the Word; nor do they accept moral limits, since it does not matter what the body does anyway. Scholars have been noticing that gnosticism fits well with today's culture and today's religious climate.[5] Modern-day Gnostics are now bolstered in their project of transcending the body and existing in a nonphysical, mental realm with the technology of the Internet.[6]

Of course, in one sense such talk of shifting identities, the rejection of the physical world, and the dissolution of reality into cyberspace is absurd. When it comes down to it, people cannot shake their true identities, nor do they really want to. Human beings can never be disembodied spirits. The desires of the flesh are behind virtual sex; pure electronic impulses should not be interested even in this vitiated and sterile variety of sensual pleasure. Such talk constitutes an ideology, not any sort of consistent practice. But it reminds us once again how human beings will do just about anything to evade God—His creation, His laws, His redemption. As human beings misuse the Internet to escape into themselves, it also reminds us of who really rules the physical universe.

INFORMATION OVERLOAD

As has been said, the Internet eliminates gatekeepers, opening the gate for Christians and other marginalized perspectives to participate in the marketplace of ideas. Nevertheless, gatekeepers perform a valuable service, and their absence on the Internet is part of its dark side.

In our postmodern mind-set, truth is relative—the construction of particular groups and individuals—so that there are no universal criteria, no objective standards by which to evaluate or judge.[7] The Internet plays right into this worldview.

On the Internet, one idea is pretty much equal to another. Though they can be argued about and flamed, all positions can have an equal presence on the Web. Search engines do not discriminate about which sites are reliable—they list them all. It is up to the user to determine what is of value. But the user often has no idea.

On the one hand, the Internet's approach to ideas seems admirably democratic and populist. On a mailing list, the participants' credentials, position, and educational background mean next to nothing and may never be known. Again, the only identity is the anonymity of the screen name. Ideas must stand on their own, in the strength of their arguments and the force of their expression. The Internet obscures the normal status markers, hierarchies, and authorities.

On the other hand, some people do have more expertise than others. There are legitimate authorities on many issues, and someone who has greater knowledge deserves a greater say. But the Internet, that great leveler, bulldozes all such distinctions.

Another problem is that the Internet favors short bullets of information. Scholarly journals and books can explore an issue in depth. But it is hard to read for long on the World Wide Web. The format favors short pieces and strong visuals. E-mail and list postings are necessarily short and casual. Chat messages must fit into little boxes. Thus much of the voluminous information available on the Web is brief, undeveloped, and ephemeral.

In the torrent of information that a user is subject to, facts, profound ideas, and insider intelligence mix freely with gossip, disinformation, and urban legends. And there is no easy way to tell which is which. The old gatekeepers were responsible for checking facts and sorting out the wheat from the chaff. Now we are on our own.

Then there is the problem of the sheer volume of information. There is so much out there. There is so much incoming. And it comes unfiltered, unorganized, in a meaningless and disorienting cascade.

This is where Christianity comes in, offering a way to make sense of the whole, to sort out right from wrong, truth from lies, and to create order out of the chaos.

Casting Your Net on the Other Side

Christianity Online

CHAPTER SEVEN

Areopagitica.com: Warfaring Christians on the Net

ฐ

So what is to be done with this medium that is so promising, yet harbors so many problems? Can the Internet be a social good despite its moral license, its solipsism, its chaos? And how can Christians, who operate from a fundamentally different worldview, function in cyberspace?

FROM A NET TO A FILTER

The nature of the medium makes it difficult, indeed impossible, to censor. Proposals have been made to outlaw the most egregious kinds of pornography and to prosecute those providers who do not keep it away from children. But the laws of a nation can hardly touch the global scope of the Internet. The Internet knows no boundaries and thus can evade every legal sovereignty.

Internet providers such as AOL do have policies by which offensive prowlers can be kicked out of accounts. But the sheer logistics of policing the millions of communications that go over the wires makes it almost impossible.

One solution is filtering software that can keep out certain negative words and sexually oriented sites. These may be a good short-term solution. Filtering software can offer a (fallible) measure of protection for children. Interestingly, companies are also buying filtering software to prevent their adult employees from spending company time downloading pornography on office computers. True, these programs can be fooled. And true, filtering software companies do not necessarily make good gate-keepers. Some filtering software will filter out Christian sites that criticize homosexuality, classifying them as "hate sites." Still, filtering software is one line of defense.

Rather than buying filtering programs for individual computers, an easier way of accomplishing the same thing may be through Internet portals. These are what come on the screen when one's Internet access is established, typically featuring news, often-used links, and features that can be customized according to the user's preferences. A number of Christian portals have been designed that will not allow access to the bad stuff.

Another way of getting at the problem may be tracking software, which records what sites have been visited. A teenager may surf the Web to his heart's content, but he will know that his parents will see a record of every place he visits. The beauty of this approach is that it reinstills the social controls of embarrassment and shame. It also puts parents in a direct supervisory role. Instead of preventing bad behavior by making it impossible, which does little to build moral character, it cultivates the conscience and teaches children to internalize their parents' values.

Again, offices are making use of tracking software to nail their employees' misuse of office equipment. It should be remembered that though immorality on the Internet is most often seen in terms of the way it harms children, it also harms adults, who often have real jobs, real marriages, and real lives that can be ruined through the temptations on the Internet. Ironically, though the Internet promises anonymity, this, like so much of cyberspace, is an illusion. It provides a virtual anonymity that seems real but is not. The fact is, nearly everything ever done on a computer can be traced and found somewhere on the hard drive. Cookies leave their trail of electronic crumbs.

Companies have every right to monitor everything that is done on their equipment, and they are increasingly cracking down on the "cyber-slackers" in their employ. It is estimated that misuse of computers costs companies $1 billion a year, not counting even more billions in lost productivity when workers are spending their time playing games or E-mailing their friends or surfing recreationally instead of attending to their jobs. So now businesses are cracking down. Twenty-seven percent of companies are now reviewing employees' E-mail, and 21 percent are checking downloaded files. At Xerox, so many people were downloading porn that the computer network became overloaded, making it impossible to send or open legitimate company E-mail. It turned out that some employees were spending their whole eight-hour day on porn sites. The company hired a team of experts to track down instances of computer abuse. Forty employees lost their jobs.[1] So social controls might come back, tempering the misuse of the Internet.

AREOPAGITICA.COM

But ultimately, technological ways of restricting access to the bad parts of technology accomplish little. "They are not skillful considerers of human things," said Milton, "who imagine to remove sin by removing the matter of sin." Making the occasion of sin more difficult does not remove the sinfulness of the human heart. "Banish all objects of lust," said Milton, "shut up all youth into the severest discipline that can be exercised in any hermitage, ye cannot make him chaste that came not thither so."[2] The only thing that can make a heart, chaste or otherwise, get at the essence of sin that lies deep within our natures and that erupts whenever it gets a chance is the Gospel of Jesus Christ, in whom alone is the forgiveness of sins and the renewal of life.

Milton was facing a similar problem with a new medium. The printing press had only been around for two centuries, but by 1644 it had created an information overload of its own. Thousands and thousands of books had come into existence, and nearly as many competing ideas. And they all had social implications. Some of them were morally questionable. Many were questioning established authorities of church and state. The ones doing the most questioning of church and state were the Puritans, Milton's own party.

The king cracked down, requiring that all books be licensed by a royal authority, who would search them for subversive sentiments before they could be published. Puritans and religious separatists who criticized the king or the established Church of England were imprisoned and could have their ears cut off. But the Puritan writings helped launch a revolution. In England the Puritans actually overthrew the king, cut off his head, and set up a republic. But in 1644 the new government put forward a licensing law of its own. Milton wrote "Areopagitica" as a plea to the republic not to revert to the old censorship that had persecuted the Puritans.

Milton argued for the freedom of the press on Christian—yes, Puritan—grounds, in full awareness of human sinfulness and the harmfulness of vice and falsehood. His whole discussion seems eerily applicable to our new communications medium. He maintained that the solution to the problems raised by the new media was not censorship but the cultivation of Christian character.

Milton pointed out that "if it comes to prohibiting, there is not aught more likely to be prohibited than truth itself."[3] He cited the most censored book of them all, censored not only by the medieval papacy but by today's liberal educators and jurists—namely, the Bible. Christians must remember that the free exchange of ideas on the Internet does, in fact, give them an opening that has long been denied them by the cultural and intellectual gatekeepers. Christians must realize that restrictions on the Internet will eventually be used to silence them. Again, think of how some filtering software is already being used to filter out Christian speech that dares to cast aspersions on homosexuality. Today's culture *likes* pornography and promiscuous sex, but it does not like Christianity. Laws to restrict content on the Internet may well end up silencing not the pornographers, but the Christians who criticize them.

Milton also, capitalist that he was, put great trust in the marketplace of ideas. He believed that free competition works not only in economics but in the struggle for truth. "Let her and falsehood grapple," he writes. "Who ever knew truth put to the worse, in a free and open encounter?"[4] He had the confidence that in competing ideas, truth would eventually win out, that when ideas are allowed to contend with each other, the best ones would survive and the phony and fallacious would die out.

Perhaps Milton was too idealistic, but surely Christians should have confidence in the strength of what they believe and confess. For all of the talk by utopians and posthumanists about freedom from the body, from the physical world, and from one's own identity, people still have an identity and a body. The physical world exists and exerts its claims, no matter how hard some people try to evade it. People may try to escape from themselves and their real-world situation on the Internet, but escape is ultimately impossible. Loners are not really accomplishing that much by retreating into virtual sex and playing pretend with their screen names. They remain miserable sinners, and they know it, though they might not admit it. Christians have reality on their side. This gives them a great advantage over every falsehood.

For Milton, the solution to the information overload and the new temptations opened up by the printing press—and by extension, the Internet—was the formation of Christian character. "He that can apprehend and consider vice with all her baits and seeming pleasures, and yet abstain, and yet distinguish, and yet prefer that which is truly better, he is the true warfaring Christian." [5]

Christians must train themselves and their children not to hide from the Internet but to resist its temptations. They must have an internalized virtue, a sanctified imagination, so that they freely choose what is good and freely reject what is evil. This is a matter of discipleship, of Christian formation.

To function on the Internet, Christians must learn to be their own gatekeepers. They must be taught, by thorough nourishment in God's Word, from a young age, the skills of discernment. Children must not only be protected—they must be taught how to fight.

"The true warfaring Christian" on the Internet will not *want* to go to those stupid porn sites. He will know himself to be a child of God, an identity that is secure and stable, so that he will not feel the need to be someone he isn't. Unlike many of his fellow surfers, he has criteria by which to judge between what is true and false, what is good and what is evil, what is beautiful and what is ugly. He becomes his own filter.

The Word of God, with the worldview it establishes,

becomes his paradigm, his means of coping with the information overload. It makes sense of the flood of data—serving as a basis for rejecting the worthless and seizing upon what is valuable, no matter what its source. And the Church—an actual community of real-life worshipers—will give him the support and the spiritual sustenance he needs, from actual people encouraging him to reach out to those he meets online.

Such a foundation should enable him to use this new tool without hurting himself (as untaught children are apt to do with power tools). He will be freed to use the tool for the good of himself and his neighbor. And this sort of grounding in the Gospel and in the Word of God will give him an advantage over all of the lost and lonely and dysfunctional computer geeks. Though he will doubtless fall short of the ideal, the renewal of the Gospel doesn't stop.

The freedom opened up by the Internet will be enjoyed in Christian freedom. The information overload will be managed by Christian discernment. The possibilities for community on the Internet will be embraced by Christian love.

CHAPTER EIGHT

The Tumbling of the Walls:
The Christian's Opportunities

§

Since the Enlightenment, Christianity has been steadily eased out of cultural influence. As long as it stays completely private and inside somebody's head, Christianity has been tolerated; but once it presumes to make truth-claims about the universe or to resist the moral decline, the cultural establishment recoils in disgust. Though Christians continue to live out their vocations in the world, across the whole gamut of talents and professions, they tend to be shut out of the role of culture-makers. Some of this is because of Christians themselves withdrawing from the world rather than taking it on. Some of this is because overt Christianity is often discriminated against in the arts, the sciences, the media, and other fields that directly shape the thought, values, and imagination of the culture as a whole.

But now, with the new information technology, nothing can keep Christians out. With all of the gatekeepers knocked out, the field is wide-open. The Internet gives Christians access to the means of cultural production. Christianity has a shot at being influential in the culture again. As the printing press was the engine of the Reformation, the Internet will be the engine of whatever comes next.

Christians can be cultural players once again. But it will take imagination, boldness, and the willingness to compete. There are opportunities to build new companies, to engage in the day's debates, and to push Christian spirituality online. There are opportunities for Christian musicians, artists, and writers to put out their work into the world. But there are also less spectacular but no less culturally important possibilities for ordinary Christians to educate their children, reform their entertainment diet, study the Scriptures, and connect together as the Church, thanks to God's gift of the Internet.

THE NEW MEDIA

The gifts of the Internet go far beyond Web browsers on desktops. Waves of new tools have sprung up from the growth of interconnectivity and fast connection. The Net is a delivery method faster than any post office or courier could ever dream. In short, a book, movie, or song can be sent over the wire without printing presses or stamps, without publishers or Hollywood studios or major recording labels. True, there are sometimes problems. Systems can slow to a crawl when too many people try to access at once, like shoppers in a crowded checkout line; and hardware limitations can mean long download times. But the hardware technology keeps improving, and these kinds of problems will soon be history.

Downloadable products can't sell out. Or wear out. They can be copied over and over perfectly. It's like software; a copy is indistinguishable from the original. Since what's being copied are binary digits sent in packets, the stock can't deplete unless the server and its hardware wears out.

It is a fact of life in the publishing industry that books, once they stop selling enough copies, go out of print. It is too expensive for a publisher to invest in the paper, manufacturing, and warehouse space unless a book can promise a reasonable return. But online, text takes up no space whatsoever, requires no trees to be cut down, and costs almost nothing. However, books will almost certainly never be obsolete, contrary to some fears. The format of multiple pages just cannot be beat by a computer screen for user-friendliness, and there will always be a need for long discourses, not just brief postings. Already, as we have seen, there are experiments in small, hand-held devices into which texts can be downloaded for easy reading. But in whatever format they appear, books—including old books—will by no means disappear. Rather, they will likely be immortalized.

Already ventures are underway by which no book need ever go out of print. The book's text will exist in a digitized form. A person can order the book, whereupon its file will be called up and custom-printed, one at a time. Mass sales—and the author's temptation to tailor the ideas to the least common denominator—will be unnecessary. Old books will be preserved and will be instantly available for anyone to rediscover. The old books that were ahead of their time and were thus ignored when they were written can wait for an audience. New books will proliferate since publishers will no longer have to see them as an investment decision. Books can be more specialized, more bold, more expressive of what the author truly thinks than ever before.

Of course, this will mean more bad books as well as more good ones. It will mean that writers will write to a niche, not to a mass market. It may result in a literary balkanization as readers segment into their separate tastes. The Internet may create communities, but it is also isolating. Having an overarching single culture may be less likely as subcultures intensify.

Nevertheless, on the whole this should be good for Christians. The great theologians of the past—many of whom are now unavailable and out of print—can be rediscovered. Christian debate and discourse will no longer have to be filtered through the demands of commercialism. The Church, which often drifts wherever the culture leads, may be able to pull itself back together and recover its own identity as the people of God. And though the Internet can build up communities, it also breaks down walls. In the new information climate, the Christian message can also extend beyond the Church in evangelism and missions.

MUSIC, MEDIA, AND MAN

Again, the Net can help cut out the middleman. It can also give products easier distribution. The new media does not simply allow communication to the like-minded; it also opens up opportunities to reach bigger and different audiences. A writer who can't get a decent book deal can sell his latest on an online bookstore like Amazon.com. Self-publishers can put their books on Amazon.com and sell them, just as Random House and HarperCollins do.

Musicians with songs but no record contract can hang out at a place like MP3.com. They might not build a mass audience, but they have an outlet for their art, and they can take a shot at a cult following.

Part of the beauty of new media is that it reshuffles the deck of cultural gatekeepers, opening the door to new voices. This applies not only to producers of cultural products, but to the people who consume them. Don't like what you hear on FM radio? Make something new. Or find a radio station from somewhere on the other side of the country that you do like by surfing through all of the stations whose broadcasts can actually be heard through the Web. Or tailor your own programming. You can access your favorite talk shows, play exactly the kind of music you want, and leaven it all with the old Jack Benny, Orson Welles, and Fibber McGee programs from the golden age of radio, all of which are available through the Web.

Don't want the usual opinions you hear from TV political commentators? Post something different. And you don't have to make your own web site to do this. You can post your views right on the mainline sites. You can talk back. Just about every major site—from CNN to NASA—has features that allow users to offer their feedback. These become forums for free, open, public discourse for individuals with an opinion. And if your arguments are sound, you may persuade the other people who are posting. Those with some diligence can get their voices heard.

Yet doing the Net isn't just like getting time on a major network. There are millions of other choices for Internet surfers to choose from. That means that to succeed, you must be more creative, dynamic, and crafty than your competitors. Most online projects get only a handful of audience members, but the potential is endless. The barriers are low, but in a universe with endless choices, getting noticed is hard work.

If you're a musician, getting noticed in the record business is a monumental task. Even great bands find the road treacherous and often don't like the contract they get when it's offered. The music business is a notorious rat race and always will be, but the Net offers a global stage for the hungry.

In the regular recording industry, even the lucky musicians who get a record deal often get frustrated. What gets released must often be the most commercial, at least as defined by the record companies at the moment, and sometimes the serious music an artist may want to make has to give way to the entertainment demands of the pop culture. Bands and fans may complain that artists must sell out to succeed, but the labels say there's a method to all this—economics. Record companies are like investment bankers and venture capitalists, putting the money in investments they think will pay off. The big hits provide cash to support the up-and-coming bands and the more sophisticated music that might not sell as much. But everything is subsidized by hit records.

The artistic problem is that manufacturing hit records makes a mass audience—not the artist—determine the nature of the work of art. Fads and fashions will carry more weight than individual creativity. Not to mention cheap thrills, the titillation of sex or violence or sentimentality, as opposed to thoughtful, subtle aesthetics. Again, music and other art forms that become commercially driven also have to appeal to the lowest common denominator; if it demands too much thinking or knowledge or if it challenges the listener too much or raises uncomfortable issues (as does Christianity), the pool of potential buyers shrinks. This is not a criticism of pop culture; it is just a fact of life.

Christian artists face even greater problems. Since the message of repentance and redemption in Christ is not often palatable to secular ears, to succeed commercially often means watering down the Christian content—or veiling it behind so much symbolism and double meaning that no one notices it. Since commercialized forms, designed mostly for pure entertainment, find it difficult, because of their innate simplicity, to carry any kind of complex or weighty meaning, even music aimed at Christian listeners often is reduced to religious pabulum. As for signing with a record company, Christian bands face a double-headed monster with religious subculture labels on one side, which are Christian-friendly but restrict one's audience to the religious subculture, and the secular labels, promising a bigger market but a hostile religious climate. Either way Christian artists are put into a position where they feel pressured to compromise either their art or their theology or both.

But it doesn't have to be this way. The new technologies open up new ways of getting heard.

For some time the music industry has been segmenting. Formerly, there was a single "hit parade," and the top stars were known by everyone. Today the old dream of being on everyone's ears is slipping away. Recorded music has diversified into numerous subgenres, each with its own dress codes and rules. That means there's more diversity in stores now than ever before. It also means you may be a rock star even though your next-door neighbor has never heard of you. Everyone used to know Frank Sinatra, Elvis, and the Beatles. But now few people outside their closed circles of adoring fans know who the latest rappers, rock and rollers, or flavor-of-the-week pop vocalists are. Even for artists who turn out to achieve great success, the mass audience is largely gone, due to such splintering.

Quick, easy distribution of music gives people too many choices, an avalanche of options that is so overwhelming, they may well choose nothing. What is happening is that new kinds of gatekeepers are emerging, people who can steer Internet users to the good stuff. These new online DJs or music sites or electronic magazines can lead people through the mess. Just like the proverbial talent scout, somebody must dig through the slush pile and see what's hot and what's not. Right now some Next Big Thing is lurking in the shadows waiting to be discovered. When some mega-success pops out of MP3-land into stardom, all sorts of new attention will go to the medium.

To deal with the information and aesthetic overload, there is thus a need for critics. And this may be an opening for Christians, applying their worldview by critiquing what is bad and teaching what is good.

Religious music in America is currently shoved into a small, cramped space largely controlled by Christian "bookstores" that generally seem to push only the most commercialized, unthoughtful product. Good stuff exists, but it is usually difficult to find without gambling a lot of money on weak albums. For those wanting more profound or less pop-oriented music, the Christian music scene is hard to navigate. The economic realities of the commercial market are inescapable. The option of punting Christian music into MP3-land may be a liberating possibility, leaving greater room than the pop scene for artistic and theological integrity. Moreover, the old line between "Christian" and "secular" music—and their different marketing schemes—can be avoided.

HAVING YOUR OWN PUBLISHING COMPANY

What goes for music also holds true for books. A Christian author faces the same dilemma as musicians, trapped between secular and sacred audiences and publishing companies. And it is just as very, very difficult to get published at all.

Self-publishing gets you a garage full of unsold copies. In most cases few authors have the marketing push to move books without a publisher. Vanity presses are often willing to spit out books for a hefty sum, but the reputation—and the marketing—from such services often isn't good.

Thus the Net is an escape route for the author without a publisher. As with music, it presents no promise of success, but it opens the door to a worldwide audience. Since readers have endless choices, getting lost in the shuffle is still a strong possibility. And if the primary goal is to make a lot of money, the conventional commercial media are definitely the way to go. But if the primary goal is to express something you think is worth saying, there are now other options.

If someone simply wants to get the word out about something, it is simply a matter of posting one's work online and giving it away. Readers can just hit the print button. Material can be published in plain text that pops up in a browser or spiffed up in formats like Adobe Acrobat that preserve typesetting. Electronic distribution can be cheap and simple. And on the horizon are the experimental machines that can take Web-based text and print real books while you wait.

Instead of first writing a book, a writer can shoot up a test flare by building a web site about his topic. This can build up a community of interested people. In effect, this is building a platform to launch a book. Essays and chapters can be tried out online to see how readers respond. And if it doesn't work, the project can be abandoned without spending the time and expense of writing a failed book.

Even self-publishing assumes a new life with the Internet. Books still usually need to be set down in ink and paper, since the electronic book will be on the drawing board for some time to come. Yet by using a well-made web site to promote a book, you can seek out your audience. Again, even if your book doesn't make it into wholesalers' warehouses, you can sign up with Amazon.com or some other online bookstore as a conduit. Much of this requires old-fashioned guerrilla marketing to succeed.

Online book and music distribution are not panaceas, but they allow the little guy to be nimble. The Internet rewards smart people, including smart Christians. While there may be only a tiny audience, there's also no gatekeeper standing somewhere keeping a certain work from finding its audience. If the decadent, immoral, and self-indulgent can use the technology, so can Christians doing groundbreaking material.

For decades the amount of quality Christian worldview work has been spotty. The secular media doesn't know what to do with it, and the religious market doesn't know how to sell it. Still, if Christians are to be salt and light, the work must be done. The Internet is a vehicle that can allow Christians to produce for each other the work they need—the theological scholarship, the critiques of the opposing worldviews, the discussion of the urgent issues before the Church—untrammeled by demands of the larger marketplace. And this same vehicle can reach those outside the walls of the Church, opening up new opportunities for apologetics, mission, and evangelism.

THE CHURCH ONLINE?

What about electronic churches? Some people have imagined whole congregations existing only online. Pastors would do their counseling in chat rooms. Evangelism calls could be made with Instant Messaging. Christian education curricula could be posted online, with small-group discussion lists taking the place of prayer groups and Bible studies. Worship would be online, with real-time video and streaming music files. (Some groups have already experimented with online liturgies, in which the members of the online congregation type in the responses.) Churches, freed from the need of having a building, could be more mega than ever before. A congregation could span the world. And no members would have the bother and inconvenience of getting up on Sunday mornings, getting dressed up, leaving the house, and having to go to church.

What is wrong with this picture? Well, as always, the Bible addresses the issue in words of challenging precision: "Let us not give up meeting together, as some are in the habit of doing, but let us encourage one another—and all the more as you see the Day approaching" (Hebrews 10:25). It may be "meeting" to log into a Christian chat room, but it is not "meeting together." The biblical model for the Church is clearly one of actual—not virtual—relationships between its members, being in each other's presence and in the presence of Christ. "For where two or three come together in my name, there am I with them" (Matthew 18:20).

Christ provided for His Church to exist through tangible activities. Baptizing with water. Reenacting His holy Supper. Listening to the preaching of His Word, in the company of the saints. The Bible describes the Church as a "body," not a disembodied spirit.

Historically, Christians have debated much about the nature of the Real Presence of Christ, alluded to in Matthew 18, how Christ is "there" in the midst of those who assemble "in my name." Many Christian traditions—Catholics, Eastern Orthodox, Lutherans—insist on the Real Presence of Christ in the bread and wine of Holy Communion. Others see this Presence as a symbolic or spiritual truth, or something happening in the hearts of the faithful. Ironically, the new issue may well involve "the real presence" of people in the congregation.

At any rate, Christians will continue to meet with each other in a literal "assembly" (which is what the Greek word for the church, *ecclesia*, means). This will be true even if everyone else gets to the point of never leaving their homes since their schooling, their work, their shopping, and their relationships are all a matter of sitting in front of a computer screen.

Once this is clear, though, and thoroughly realized, the Church can indeed establish a presence (of a sort) online. Today denominations have their own homepages, which can be invaluable in communicating with their members—posting theological statements, directories of congregations and clergy, denominational news and announcements. Local churches too have their web pages, posting everything from the ushering schedule to the pastor's sermons. The Internet can inform, mobilize, and unify congregations and church bodies.

There are also sites online designed to aid the study of the Bible. There are sites for heavy-duty theological scholarship and apologetics. Various parachurch organizations are on the Web. Many publications and periodicals can be found free on the Web, and one can do research into specific issues with the help of online databases and search engines. There are Christian portals that include filtering systems to keep out the bad things on the Internet while identifying what is valuable. Christian sites can be tied together with hyperlinks, so that, say, someone interested in pro-life activism can jump from one set of allies to another.

Then there are the less formal lists of Christian friends, Christians interested in the same topic, and Christians laboring in the same vocation. These can offer valuable mutual support and admonition. Members can discuss theology, delve into matters they are trying to understand, ask about how to handle problems, and pray for each other.

The Web can literally link Christians together. That this strengthens Christians—and real churches—goes without saying. It can also be a forum for thinking Christianly, for working out controversies, and for service in the world.

The Web is no panacea, and it can create problems of its own. Though it is a chaotic place, it is wide-open. Christians would do well to get in on the ground floor.

CHAPTER NINE

Conclusion:
Gutenberg Squared

⑤

So, are the vast and perilous reaches of cyberspace any place for Christians? What does God have to do with cyberspace?

Many different kinds of communications media have emerged over the centuries, each with its different challenges and possibilities. For the most part Christianity has made good use of them all. While the newly emerging communication technology promises to do much to change the social and intellectual landscape, Christians can use the new technology—as they have others—to multiply and promulgate the Word of God. Faced with information overload, Christians can build a filtering and structuring mechanism of their own—a biblical worldview. And they can use the new technology to influence the culture once again.

CHRISTIANITY AND MEDIA

When the relatively new information technology of books hit ancient Greece, Plato was concerned. If reading and writing catch on, he warned, they will have a detrimental effect. Human beings will lose their capacity for memory. Instead of internalizing the information they need, people will just write it down, to consult as needed. Education will degenerate. Instead of learning *The Iliad* and *The Odyssey* by heart, children will just put it on the shelf. The intellect will shrink as knowledge becomes stored outside the human mind.

Plato was the first media critic. Although it might seem easy to assume that Plato was overreacting—an example of the crotchety Luddite prophet of doom who seems to accompany all revolutionary new technologies—the fact remains that Plato was right. People in literate societies do seem to lack the memory capacity of those in oral cultures. African tribesmen can still exhibit prodigious feats of memory, reciting seemingly endless genealogies and thousands of lines of tribal epics, while those of us who can read and write rely on Post-its to remind us what to pick up at the grocery store. New information media do affect the way people think, the possibilities of a culture, and its worldview.

There are trade-offs. It is true and unfortunate that the sum total of human knowledge is stored in libraries rather than in our heads. And yet the ability to store language (writing) and to decode it (reading) means that knowledge can accumulate in ways impossible where language is merely spoken. Tribal societies tend to stay basically the same from age to age, with each generation reenacting the life-cycle of the generation gone before. The lore of the past is memorized and passed on, but individual discoveries or new ideas die with the person who thought them up. Each generation is starting over, repeating the past, as it were, by memory.

In literate cultures, on the other hand, ideas can be saved. The great idea of one individual can be drawn upon by someone who has not had that idea. Discoveries build upon discoveries. No one who can read has to start over from scratch. The wheel does not have to be reinvented, since its specifications and its physics and the technology for engineering it are thoroughly documented. New things, over the years, can be added to the wheel, such as internal combustion engines, automatic transmissions, and cupholders. The West's technological progress and intellectual wealth are directly related to the invention of writing and reading.

Plato was correct to see that the worldview of his beloved Greece, with its idealized tribal virtues, would be undermined by the rise of books. But this new information technology would fit well with the worldview of the ancient Hebrews, who believed that God communicates to human beings not primarily through ecstatic visions or human representatives or cultural institutions but through a Book. The Hebrew Bible, in fact, goes back to the origins of writing itself. And the alphabet we use today—which, by breaking down the sounds of speech into discrete visible symbols, makes reading and writing both possible and easily learned—was the invention of an ancient Middle Eastern people mentioned in Scripture, the Phoenicians, whose Semitic language is related to Hebrew.

Christianity brought God's Word—and with it schools, literacy, and other kinds of books—wherever it went, soon displacing the tribal gods of European paganism and their oral traditions. But books had to be copied by hand, a laborious and expensive process. Bibles, lovingly illuminated and gilded, were honored, but they were rare. Many churches could not even afford a Bible. And those that did often kept it chained to the altar, so it could not be stolen. And of the few people who were privileged enough to own a Bible, still fewer could read it. The clergy were taught to read, but not many others. Even kings and the aristocracy were often illiterate. No wonder the church of the Middle Ages drifted away from biblical truth.

The Reformation made God's Word central. The Bible was to be the source and norm of all doctrine and conduct, the means by which the Holy Spirit communicates the good news of Jesus Christ and creates faith in the human heart. The Reformation was accompanied by—and made possible by—the second major information revolution and the first to be animated by technology: the printing press.

Others before Luther had sought to reemphasize the Scriptures, had criticized practices of the medieval church, and had taught that salvation is a free gift of God through Jesus Christ. But they could be simply burned at the stake and thus silenced. But by Luther's time Gutenberg had invented the printing press, writings could be mass-produced, and ordinary people had learned to read them. Luther's 95 Theses against the sale of indulgences were printed as broadsides and spread, seemingly overnight, across northern Europe. What had been posted on a single church door was now in the hands of thousands. Though an attempt was made to silence Luther in the usual way, his ideas were in print, circulating and changing the way people were thinking.

Then, while in hiding from his inquisitors, Luther used his time to translate the entire Bible into the language of the people. And that Bible was mass-produced, coming off printing presses by the tens of thousands. Mass production meant that it could be manufactured relatively cheaply. It wasn't long before nearly every family in Germany, including the peasants, had a Bible in their home. In the meantime, other vernacular translations were made and mass-produced in other countries, and the Reformation churches opened schools to ensure that everyone could read them. In the process, lives were changed as the Word of God—now preached from the pulpits and read at home—convicted people of sin and converted them to faith in Christ.

Luther himself credited the success of the Reformation to God's providential design in raising up the printing press. "I did nothing," he would say in essence. He and Melanchthon (his collaborator, an expert in the ancient languages) just put the Word out. While they were sitting around in Wittenberg, he would say, the Word of God did it all. But it was the printing press—the first mass medium, the first large-scale information technology—that promulgated that Word. And today's information technology is nothing more than an acceleration of what the printing press started.

As new communication technologies were developed, they too were co-opted by the Church to proclaim God's Word. The telegraph bound the world together, so people could read about what was happening in the far corners of the earth. This shrinkage of the globe was surely a factor in the rise of global missions in the nineteenth century.

Radio proved to be a particularly successful medium for Christians, enabling them—from the technology's very beginning—to broadcast sermons, teaching, and evangelism outside of churches and into people's homes. Even today Christian radio is a significant voice on the airwaves.

The Church has been somewhat less successful in conveying its message through the new visual media. Christianity has a long tradition of drama—in fact, our nonclassical western drama is an invention of the Church, whose acting out of Bible stories in the mystery plays during the Middle Ages led in a direct line to today's dramas in New York and Hollywood. There have been some powerful religious movies, from silent classics to the searching symbolism of Bergman's *The Seventh Seal*. But Christians have often been leery of the film world, due to culture war clashes, and have tended to leave the making of movies to the entertainment industry.

Television has been even more difficult for Christians to use effectively. Though there have been no shortage of TV ministries, television is such a powerful entertainment medium that it has sometimes distorted the message of the Cross.[1] The phrase "TV evangelist" has, often unfairly, conjured up images of phoniness, religious commercialism, and shallow theology. The downfall of several TV preachers due to adultery and fraud has reinforced this impression. To be sure, many Christians have made good use of TV, but there is surely much more that can be done.

One problem may be that television is intrinsically a visual medium, while Christianity is a religion of the Word. The conflict between image-based religions and word-based religions is as old at the Old Testament. As Neil Postman has shown, images tend to be emotional, fragmented, anti-intellectual, and immediate, whereas language is rational, connected, abstract, and unfolding.[2] The faith of the Hebrews and the Christians, grounded in an invisible, transcendent God who could not be captured in a tangible image, was very different from that of their Canaanite neighbors, whose gods were embodied in stone and were worshiped in orgiastic rites. Certainly Christianity— which teaches that God, who created the physical universe and declared it good, became flesh in Jesus Christ—values concreteness and, in contrast to eastern and gnostic spirituality, values the physical. But it remains a religion grounded in language, the Word of God. Since TV includes words, it would seem that Christianity might make some sort of peace with this particular medium.

Postman is a harsh critic of the electronic media, including the Internet. But in his earlier writings calling into question the educational potential of television, on the grounds that images cannot convey ideas in the way language can, Postman held out rather more hope for the newly emerging computer technology. Computers, he said, tend to be language-oriented. Computers have to be programmed with a *language*. And much of the information they store is *text*.[3]

Even today cyberspace consists largely of language. Across the world people are typing words into their computers. What they find on the Web must be read. Certainly the Internet is now also a realm of images, with 3-D effects, streaming video, and virtual-reality illusions. The synthesis of television and the Web will soon, we are told, be achieved.

But insofar as the Internet is an *information* medium—as opposed to an entertainment or an experiential medium, which it is also becoming—it will remain grounded in language. There is no other way for human beings to encode information, express their thoughts, and communicate to other people. The capacity to do all of these things is what language is. As scholars are showing, language underlies all thought, all culture, and all personal relationships. It is irreplaceable. As long as the Internet is, among other things, a language medium, it can be a forum for God's Word.

THE INTERNET AND THE GUTENBERG TRADITION

A major effect of the continuing Gutenberg revolution has been the democratization of information. The printing press put books in the hands of everyone. The literacy rate skyrocketed, and men, women, and children of every social class were taught how to read the Bible. And once they knew how to read the Bible, they could read anything. A peasant boy could now have access to the best ideas of the ages and the most useful information of his time. He could sharpen his mind, meaning that he was not necessarily held down anymore by his humble origins. With more or less universal education came the rise of the middle class. Businesses, investments, trade, and new inventions flourished. The old-line aristocracy soon had to borrow money from the commoners.

Once ordinary citizens became educated, having access to information by means of their literacy, they acquired political power. Ordinary folk now could become well-informed about the issues of the day, thanks to the printing press making possible the art of journalism. They were even empowered to criticize their leaders since they held in their hands a higher authority, the Holy Bible. They could participate in public discourse, which led to participation in public policy. It took a while, but eventually democratic republics displaced the absolute monarchies.

To be sure, the move to democracy came at the cost of social instability. Demagogues could manipulate the masses, the majority could exercise a tyranny of its own, and the allure of the least common denominator could result in a culture of mediocrity—just as the classical critics of democracy had warned. But still, for better or worse, the net result has been the growth of individual freedom and opportunity unparalleled in the days of rigid class hierarchies, which were smashed by the power of the printing press.

Today the Internet takes the democratization of information to new levels. An individual with a computer can now tap into a vast reservoir of information that was once impossible to get—business data, government documents, scientific studies, news sources from around the world. Unlike what the printing press could do, this information can be completely up to date and accessible instantly. Since people can bypass the officially sanctioned and officially controlled dispensers of information, controlling people through propaganda—a necessity for tyrants—is now more difficult. Since people can access such a wide range of opinions, they can think for themselves, and so tyranny is more difficult.

If knowledge is power, individuals are indeed being empowered by the new technology. Like the uncharted "new world" opened up by Renaissance explorers, the Internet opens up a host of economic opportunities—from killings on the stock market to "killer applications" to buying and selling in virtual stores that exist only in cyberspace.

The printing press, for all of its virtues, retained an element of information control. The person who owned the press controlled what got printed. Not all of the bright ideas got published. Some were deemed unworthy of dissemination. Others were considered not salable. Publishers—whether individuals or corporations and academic institutions—became gatekeepers and shapers of the intellectual climate. The great catalyst for political discourse was freedom of the press, but not everyone owned a press.

With the new technology, everyone can, in effect, own their own press. Treatises, fiction, opinions, and rants can be posted on the Web, sent out via E-mail, and disseminated by endless forwards.

In E-mail lists and chat rooms, ordinary folk are participating in discussions, arguments, and exploratory conversations about whatever concerns them. The great debates used to be waged at the general store, or witnessed like spectator sports as statesmen like Lincoln and Douglas would square off, or followed by reading letters to the editor or dueling articles in academic journals. Now they are waged over the Internet. And though experts can discuss their ideas among their peers, there is a wider participation now than was possible before, participation on a personal level as individuals thousands of miles away from each other hammer out issues over E-mail.

Even the academic gatekeeping of degree-granting, credentialing, and the reputation of authority gets bypassed. In the anonymity of the Internet, one person's ideas have the same standing as another's, making for a true democracy of ideas.

Not that this is all necessarily good. Crackpots mingle with the knowledgeable, and as bad ideas, hoaxes, urban legends, and lies are mixed indistinguishably from facts, knowledge, and truth, it is increasingly difficult to determine which is which. Nevertheless, we are closer to a true marketplace of ideas in which, as Milton dreamed, truth and falsehood can contend with each other, with truth ultimately driving out the lies.

Throughout the modern era, no other way of thinking has been more marginalized and kept out of consideration by the information gatekeepers than Christianity. Academia has often excluded supernatural claims with methodological rigor. No mainline biology journal would print any kind of evidence for creation as opposed to evolution. Christian artists could often not get exhibited. Christian fiction writers had trouble getting published. Christianity was kept in its narrow boxes of theology and church and not allowed to "contaminate" the intellectual or cultural establishment as a whole.

But now Christian art, literature, research, and arguments can find free expression and interchange on the Web. They can be posted and thus preserved for others to see and use. Christians can enter into debates they might normally be excluded from. Christianity can contend in the marketplace of ideas.

The Internet is not only more participatory, it is more personal than the printing press. Christians should appreciate how the Internet promotes human connections. To be sure, these can be phony and exploitive, but they can also be genuine. A virtual community is still a kind of community. Modernism fragmented human relationships and undermined communal values, but the Internet, to a certain extent, can put some of them back together. People used to live as adults in the same communities into which they were born, tied closely to their extended families and life-long friends. The mobility and job pressures of the twentieth century shattered these relationships, so that children moved far away from their parents, and friendships became disposable. Today people are still extraordinarily mobile, but parents can keep in close touch with their far-flung children every day by checking their E-mail, and friendships can be maintained no matter how far away people are from each other.

Virtual communities of Christians are no substitute for life within an actual church, any more than disembodied E-mail friendships can take the place of flesh-and-blood relationships. But at the same time it would be wrong to diminish the mutual prayers, support, and edification that are taking place via the Internet. A typical Christian E-mail list might include Christians from around the world, all interacting and praying and studying with each other, modeling, in effect, the communion of the saints.

These wide and varied personal contacts made possible by the new technology also provide Christians an opportunity to inter-act with non-Christians and to explain to them the Gospel of Jesus Christ. E-mail conversations can become quite personal very quickly, their very anonymity allowing a level of intimacy impossible in most face-to-face social situations. Moral issues, personal problems, and questions of worldview arise in the natural course of things. It becomes easy to talk about spiritual matters. This needs to be done not as "Christian spam"—mass-mailed canned testimonies or, more usually, vindictive condemnations to hell, which the Net world universally finds annoying, unpersuasive, and denigrating to the Christian faith. Rather, evangelism can hap-

pen in the context of a personal interchange—clearing up mis-
conceptions about Christianity, explaining how the God we worship became incarnate in Christ and how He offers salvation not
through a legalistic set of requirements as non-Christian netizens
tend to assume but as a free gift, a forgiveness won by the Christ
on the cross.

Certainly the Internet gives full play to human depravity.
Hate and perversions and lust and cruelties make up a huge part
of the Internet landscape. This shouldn't surprise Christians,
who understand the depths of sinfulness in human nature better than anyone else. Christians must contend with the evils of
the Internet not only by protecting their children from its dangers in an external way, but, more effectively, by recovering the
age-old disciplines of fighting temptation, developing Christian
character, and living a life of sanctification. Christians need to
build a moral presence on the Internet.

The printing press too was misused, mass-producing not
only Bibles but pornography, propaganda, and a whole succes-
sion of false, atheistic philosophies. But Christians found ways
to use the press to build the Church. This new media poses similar problems and problems of its own, perhaps on a bigger
scale. As a tool it is neutral, with the capacity to be used for good
or for evil. Christians *can* use it, just as we have learned to use
the printing press.

GOD IN CYBERSPACE

The world of cyberspace is indeed a human construction. Made
possible by human technology, it is populated by sheer cre-
ations of the human mind. Ingenious ideas, artistic expressions,
visual illusions, and grotesque sinful fantasies make up the
Internet universe.

It is, of course, a pale imitation of the real world—the one made by God—which is objective, solid, rich, and multifaceted. Many people reject the created universe in favor of the one they can create for themselves, and so they withdraw into solipsism, a process made easier and more entertaining by the Internet. The cyberworld can be in relationship to the real world insofar as it records objective truth. But in its nature it is very much a human world, a sort of extended mind. The problems of cyberspace are those of the human heart, now projected into a global, multi-participatory network.

So even if it is lawful for Christians to participate in this all-too human network, is God really present there as well?

The answer is that God is present in the midst of this virtual world just as He is present in the real world that He upholds and sustains. He is present in His Word—the Word written, the Word proclaimed, the Word incarnate. "God's Word is the treasure that sanctifies all things," said Luther. "At whatever time God's Word is taught, preached, heard, read, or pondered, there the person, the day, and the work are sanctified by it, not on account of the external work but on account of the Word which makes us all saints."[4]

As Christians enter into cyberspace in their vocations, using their God-given talents, inclinations, and opportunities, as they use the new information technology as a tool to ponder and promote God's Word, and as they form Christian communities throughout the Web, God will break into this human world—as He has always done—to bring redemption.

Bibliography

Anuff, Joey and Ana M. Cox, eds. *Suck: Worst-Case Scenarios in Media, Culture, Advertising, and the Internet*. San Francisco: Hardwired, 1997.

Barber, Benjamin R. *Jihad vs. McWorld*. New York: Times Books, 1995.

Bennahum, David S. *Extra Life: Coming of Age in Cyberspace*. New York: Basic Books, 1998.

Bloom, Harold. *The American Religion: The Emergence of the Post-Christian Nation*. New York: Simon & Schuster, 1992.

Canter, Laurence A. and Martha A. Siegel. *How to Make a Fortune on the Information Superhighway*. New York: HarperCollins, 1995.

Coupland, Douglas. *Microserfs*. New York: HarperCollins, 1994.

Davis, Erik. *TechGnosis: Myth, Magic & Mysticism in the Age of Information*. New York: Harmony Books, 1998.

Dent, Harry S. *The Roaring 2000s*. New York: Simon & Schuster, 1999.

Dertouzos, Michael. *What Will Be: How the New World of Information Will Change Our Lives*. San Francisco: Harper, 1997.

Gelernter, David. *Machine Beauty: Elegance and the Heart of Technology*. New York: Basic Books, 1998.

Gershenfeld, Neil. *When Things Start to Think*. New York: Henry Holt & Company, 1999.

Gilder, George. *Life After Television: The Coming*

Transformation of Media and American Life, revised edition. New York: W.W. Norton, 1994.

Godwin, Mike. *Cyber Rights: Defending Free Speech in the Digital Age*. Times Books, 1998.

Hayles, Katherine. *How We Became Posthuman: Virtual Bodies in Cybernetics, Literature, and Informatics*. Chicago; University of Chicago Press, 1999.

Horton, Michael. *In the Face of God*. Dallas: Word, 1996.

Huber, Peter. *Orwell's Revenge: The 1984 Palimpset*. New York: The Free Press, 1994.

Hyman, Michael. *PC Roadkill: Twisted Tales from Silicon Valley*. Foster City, CA: IDG Books, 1995.

Lessard, Bill and Steve Baldwin. *Net Slaves: True Tales of Working the Web*. New York: McGraw-Hill, 2000.

Lifton, Robert Jay. *The Protean Self*. Chicago: University of Chicago Press, 1999.

Moore, Geoffrey, Paul Johnson, and Tom Kippola. *The Gorilla Game*. New York: HarperCollins, 1998.

Myers, Kenneth. *All God's Children and Blue Suede Shoes: Christians and Popular Culture*. Wheaton, IL: Crossway Books, 1989.

Norman, Donald A. *The Invisible Computer: Why Good Products Can Fail, the Personal Computer Is So Complex, and Information Appliances Are the Solution*. Cambridge, MA: MIT Press, 1998.

O'Donnell, James J. *Avatars of the Word: From Papyrus to Cyberspace*. Cambridge, MA: Harvard University Press, 1998.

Olasky, Marvin. *Prodigal Press*. Wheaton, IL: Crossway Books, 1988.

Postman, Neil. *Amusing Ourselves to Death: Public Discourse in the Age of Show Business.* New York: Viking, 1985.

—. *Technopoly: The Surrender of Culture to Technology.* New York: Vintage Books, 1992.

Rheingold, Howard. *The Virtual Community: Homesteading on the Electronic Frontier.* Reading, MA: Addison Wesley, 1993.

Rucker, Rudy et al. *Mondo 2000: A User's Guide to the New Edge.* New York: Harper Perennial, 1992.

Rushkoff, Douglas. *Media Virus: Hidden Agendas in Popular Culture.* New York: Ballantine, 1994.

Schilder, Klaas. *Christ and Culture.* Winnipeg: Premier, 1977.

Schneier, Bruce. *Applied Cryptography* (2nd Edition). New York: John Wiley & Sons, Inc., 1995.

Seabrook, John. *Deeper: My Two-Year Odyssey in Cyberspace.* New York: Simon & Schuster, 1997.

Segaller, Stephen. *Nerds 2.0.1: A Brief History of the Internet.* New York: TV Books, 1998.

Shenk, David. *Data Smog: Surviving the Information Glut.* New York: HarperCollins, 1997.

Shulman, Seth. *Owning the Future.* Boston: Houghton Mifflin, 1999.

St. Jude, R. U. Sirius, and Bart Nagel. *The Cyberpunk Handbook.* New York: Random House, 1995.

Stoll, Clifford. *Silicon Snake Oil: Second Thoughts on the Information Highway.* New York: Doubleday, 1995.

Toffler, Alvin. *The Third Wave.* New York: Bantam, 1980.

Van Til, Henry R. *The Calvinistic Concept of Culture.* Grand Rapids, MI: Baker, 1972.

Veith, Gene Edward, Jr. *Postmodern Times: A Christian Guide* to *Contemporary Thought and Culture*. Wheaton, IL: Crossway Books, 1994.

Wertheim, Margaret. *The Pearly Gates of Cyberspace: A History of Space from Dante to the Internet*. New York: W.W. Norton, 1999.

Wingren, Gustaf. *Luther on Vocation*. Evanston, IN: Ballast Press, 1994.

Wolf, Michael J. *The Entertainment Industry: How Mega Media Forces Are Transforming Our Lives*. New York: Times Books, 1999.

Wolff, Michael. *Burn Rate: How I Survived the Gold Rush Years on the Internet*. New York: Simon & Schuster, 1998.

Notes

Chapter One:
Introduction: The Latest Frontier

1 Martha Mendoza, "New Survey Shows Unwanted E-Mail Proliferating," Associated Press wire story, June 14, 1999.

2 "ISPs and Spam: The Impact of Spam on Customer Retention and Acquisition," GartnerGroup Report published at http://www.brightmail.com/company/media/gartner/.

3 Quoted in Jon Katz, "Selfish Society," *Slashdot*, August 1, 2000. See http://slashdot.org/features/00/07/24/202207.shtml.

4 Interview with Frank Gregorsky excerpted in *Speaking of George Gilder* (Seattle: Discovery Institute, 1998), p. 219.

5 Erik Davis, *TechGnosis: Myth, Magic & Mysticism* (New York: Harmony Books, 1998).

Chapter Two:
What Hath God Wrought: The History of the Computer

1 Stephen E. Ambrose, *Undaunted Courage: Meriwether Lewis, Thomas Jefferson, and the Opening of the American West* (New York: Simon & Schuster, 1996), p. 52.

2 Ibid., p. 53.

3 Computers keep getting cheaper, but not everyone wants to shell out another thousand dollars to run the latest software. That calls for tweaking. Once upon a time enthusiasts would pop the hoods of their Fords and Chevies and tinker around for new ways to put more pep in the old V8. Today their descendants by the thousands pull the cases off the PCs and play with tiny switches on circuit boards to get more power out of their Pentiums. The practice is called overclocking, meaning that computer owners search for ways to make their PC's processor move faster. Who cares about violating that old warranty anyway? Flipping little jumper switches sometimes works, even if it can cause problems. Overclocking the process can make the computer run faster—and hotter, causing it to crash and burn. It also can shorten the chip's life and make it die earlier. Yet this is worth the risk, because tinkering is free while upgrades cost money. New software is written for speedier machines, leaving the old standbys behind. Thus overclocking becomes tantalizing to the techie-inclined who are stuck with a slow computer that still has payments left.

4 David E. Kalish, "IBM Pulls PCs out of U.S. Stores," Associated Press wire story, October 19, 1999.

5 Donald A. Norman, *The Invisible Computer* (Cambridge, MA: MIT Press, 1998), p. 52.

6 David Gelernter, *Machine Beauty* (New York: Basic Books, 1998), p. 23.

7 Ibid., p. 129.

8 Ibid., p. 132.

Chapter Three:
Networking: The Community Technology

1 Richard Carelli, "Court Backs Internet Providers," Associated Press wire story, May 1, 2000.

2 Matthew Fordahl, "Internet's 30th Birthday Celebrated," Associated Press wire story, September 3, 1999.

3 Jeff Donn, "Fantasy Games Spyr Real-World Trade," Associated Press wire story, July 30, 2000.

4 Kathleen O'Toole, "Study Takes Early Look at Social Consequences of Net Use," Stanford Online Report, February 16, 2000, http://www.stanford.edu/dept/news/report/news/february16/internetsurvey-216.html.

5 Ibid.

Chapter Four:
The Weaving of the Web: The Realm of the Hyperlink

1 Jeff Donn, "'Map' of a Human Chromosome Is Drawn for the First Time," *The Milwaukee Journal*, December 2, 1999, p. 3A.

2 "Doughnut Co. Buys Site for Gripes," Associated Press wire story, August 26, 1999.

3 "Gender Gap Exists in Internet Usage," PC Data press release, September 1, 1999. See http://www.pcdataonline.com/press/pcdo 9199.asp.

4 Another overstated case for online government intervention involves the so-called "digital divide." The term is used in political circles to drag class warfare onto the Internet with visions of upscale techie elites depriving the underprivileged of their slice of digital prosperity. The Internet is like broadcast TV, radio, and the alarm clock. It will be universal soon enough with or without government help.

5 Jesse J. Holland, "Killer Punished After eBay Sales," Associated Press wire story, September 18, 1999.

6 Tricia Serju-Harris, "eBay Interrupts Houston's Firm Stock Auction," *Houston Chronicle*, September 9, 1999.

7 "Wendy's Sues over Web Site Names," Associated Press wire story, September 10, 1999.

8 Napster became the vanguard of what became known as Peer-to-Peer (P2P) computing. With this type of system, someone uses software like a search engine to find what he wants. Then the two parties make a transaction. With millions and millions of people using computers, the ability to go digging this way becomes more valuable as time passes. Many fear that a boom in P2P-type computing will result in a world of "dot-communism" where anything from pop music to nuclear bomb secrets are free-floating on the Net, open to anyone and virtually untraceable.

The whole Napster affair challenged the state of intellectual property worldwide: If someone makes a book, song, or movie a piece of software, in what sense does he "own" it? What right does he have to make money for the effort when new copies are created? What happens if copyright laws can be easily ignored because copying and redistribution is available at the click of a mouse?

9 Peter Svensson and Seth Sutel, "Publishers Closer to E-Book Sales," Associated Press wire story, May 24, 2000.

10 King's other curiosity twist was whether people would read a book online if they got it in short installments. The prototypical form of serialized writing is the sermon. Numerous churches post their pastor's weekly message online for others to read. The distribution is simple, cheap, and extends far beyond the confines of a local parish.

11 Quoted from "The Genesis of the CCEL," http://www.ccel.org/info/ccel-story.html.

12 Amazingly, the Weblogs are often indistinguishable from one another except in design. The same links can spread like a virus from one to others.

Chapter Five:
The Internet as a Conserving Activity

1 Alan Murray, "The Economy Is New; Human Nature Isn't," *The Wall Street Journal*, May 24, 1999, p. A1.

2 The term is used in Jacob M. Schlesinger, "If E-Commerce Helps Inflation, Why Did Prices Just Spike?" *The Wall Street Journal*, October 18, 1999, p. A8.

3 Murray, "The Economy Is New; Human Nature Isn't," p. A1.

4 Schlesinger, "If E-Commerce Helps Inflation, Why Did Prices Just Spike?" p. A1.

5 Ibid.

6 Quoted in Michael Ruby, "Internet Economy Will Dwarf the Industrial Revolution," *Milwaukee Journal Sentinel*, October 31, 1999, p. 3J.

7 Quoted in ibid.

8 Schlesinger, "If E-Commerce Helps Inflation, Why Did Prices Just Spike?" p. A1.

9 Kevin Maney, "High-yield Crop: E-commerce Sets Roots into Agriculture," *USA Today*, November 17, 1999, p. 3B.

10 Quoted in Haya El Nasser, "Main Street Enters Mainstream," *USA Today*, November 16, 1999, p. 3A.

11 Fred Wilber of Buch Spieler Music in Montpelier, VT, quoted in ibid.

12 Maureen Blaney Flietner, "Internet Film Reviews Open New Doors for Librarian," *Milwaukee Journal Sentinel*, November 1, 1999, p. 2B.

13 Thomas L. Friedman, "Even You Can Be Amazon.com, Come to Think of It," *New York Times* syndication, in *The Milwaukee Journal Sentinel*, March 1, 1999, p. 8A.

14 Nancy Pearcey, "Rediscovering Parenthood in the Information Age," *The Family in America*, A Publication of the Rockford Institute Center on the Family in America, 8 (March 1994), pp. 1-10.

Chapter Six:
The Dark Side of the Internet

1 John Leland, "More Buck for the Bang: How Sex Has Transformed the Porn Industry," *Newsweek*, September 20, 1999, p. 61.

2 *Exposition of Psalm 147* (1532). See Gustaf Wingren, *Luther on Vocation* (Evanston, IN: Ballast Press, 1994), p. 138.

3 See Robert Jay Lifton, *The Protean Self* (Chicago: University of Chicago Press, 1999).

4 See Katherine Hayles, *How We Became Posthuman: Virtual Bodies in Cybernetics, Literature, and Informatics* (Chicago: University of Chicago Press, 1999).

5 See Harold Bloom, *The American Religion: The Emergence of the Post Christian Nation* (New York: Simon & Schuster, 1992) and Michael Horton, *In the Face of God* (Dallas: Word, 1996).

6 See Erik Davis, *TechGnosis: Myth, Magic & Mysticism in the Age of Information* (New York: Harmony Books, 1998).

7 See Gene Edward Veith, *Postmodern Times: A Christian Guide to Contemporary Thought and Culture* (Wheaton, IL: Crossway, 1994).

Chapter Seven:
Areopagitica.com: Warfaring Christians on the Net

1 Keith Naughton, "Cyberslacking: The Internet Has Brought Distractions into Cubicles, and Now Corporate America Is Fighting Back," *Newsweek*, November 29, 1999, p. 64.

2 John Milton, "Areopagitica," in *The Student's Milton*, ed. Frank Allen Patterson (New York: Appleton-Century-Crofts, 1957), p. 741.

3 Ibid., p. 752.

4 Ibid., p. 751.

5 Ibid., p. 738.

Chapter Nine:
Conclusion: *Gutenberg Squared*

1 See Neil Postman, *Amusing Ourselves to Death: Public Discourse in the Age of Show Business* (New York: Viking, 1985), pp. 116-121.

2 Neil Postman, *Teaching as a Conserving Activity* (New York: Delacorte Press, 1979), pp. 47-70. Postman also distinguishes between the image-oriented Canaanite and the word-oriented Hebrews in *Amusing Ourselves to Death*, p. 9ff.

3 Postman, *Teaching as a Conserving Activity*, pp. 15-25, 129ff.

4 "The Large Catechism of Dr. Martin Luther," in *The Book of Concord*, ed. Theodore G. Tappert (Philadelphia: Fortress Press, 1959), p. 377.

Index

Abacus, the, 31, 32
Adobe Acrobat, 155
Advanced Micro Devices, 38
Aiken, Howard, 35
Altair, 36
Amazon.com, 9, 83, 106, 122, 152, 155
Ambrose, Stephen, 29
America Online, 13, 14, 56, 62, 65, 125, 141
Analytical engine, the, 33
"Anonymity" online, 14, 78, 79, 109, 128, 137, 143
APB Online, 92
Apple computers, 36, 37, 44, 54
Applewhite, Marshall, 20
Aptiva, 38, 39
"Areopagitica" (Milton), 144
ARPA (Department of Defense Advanced Research Projects Agency), 53
ARPANET, 53, 57
Associated Press, the, 31
Atari, 36, 37, 54
Auctions online, 9, 10, 82, 117
Autobytel, 81
AutoNation, 81

Babbage, Charles, 33
Balaam, 47, 48
Bandwidth, 17, 18
Barbie PC, the, 40
Barua, Anitesh, 118
Bauhaus, 46
Bell, Alexander Graham, 53
Bergman, Ingmar, 165
Berners-Lee, Tim, 72, 73, 97

Bible software, 96, 160
Biblical or Christian worldview, 26, 102, 109, 127, 153, 155, 161
Borsook, Paulina, 16
Bowlin, Lyle, 121, 122
Brand, Stewart, 57
Broadband transmission, 43
Broadcasting, 15, 112
Buddy lists, 13
Bulletin boards (BBS), 52, 54, 55, 56, 58, 59, 60, 62, 65, 68
Business 2.0, 18

Calculator, the, 32, 35, 36, 44
Canter, Lawrence, 63
Capek, Karel, 34
CarPoint, 81
CarsDirect.com, 81
CBBS (Computer Bulletin Board System), 54
Cell phones, 44
Censorship, 52, 55, 105, 141, 144, 145
Centipede, 37
Chat rooms, 13, 14, 19, 50, 56, 61, 65, 68, 94, 125, 129, 134, 135, 137, 156, 169
China, 111
Christensen, Ward, 54
Christian Classics Ethereal Library, 89
Christian freedom, 104, 127, 147
Christianity, Christians online, see esp. 98, 141 (Chapter 7 *passim*), 150
Clinton, President William, 110
CNN, 153